Life Interrupted  accessible, prac former creative (who has himself suffered and struggled with these very themes. I particularly appreciate the vulnerability with which Andrew shares, and the thoughtful 'Interrupter' exercises he provides at the end of each chapter. This feels more like a series of coffee-dates with a wise and kind mentor, than a succession of earnest chapters for the religiously inclined. It is, in other words, precisely the kind of interruption we all need!

Pete Greig, founder of 24-7 Prayer International and Emmaus Rd

An old Yiddish proverb, "We plan, and God laughs," reminds us that our best-laid plans for life can be upended by the unwanted, unknown, and unplanned. God laughs not to mock but because he knows his plans to bless us within the interruptions to life. This book is a most helpful and hopeful guide to understanding why God is present in the intrusions and disruptions of life and how to find more of him through those. Let Andrew, who wonderfully found God in his interruptions, be your companion and guide as you discover where God is present in yours.

Jason Swan Clark, Principal and Head of Waverley Abbey College

"A comfortable life is a myth" is a brilliant line from Andrew's warm, wry, and conversational book for those attempting to follow the Spirit, the Perfect Interrupter. It's filled with insights on how our hyper-speed lifestyles can be – or need be – kiboshed, slowed down, or rerouted by disruptions, divine and otherwise. With gracious humility, he describes his own foibles and, as common to all us carbon-based bipeds, his drive for performance, approval, and the internal forces that cause us to lose sight of the God of peace. Andrew follows each chapter with beautiful prayers and reflective ideas to give our minds margin and respite. This is the perfect book for those of us who wince at the dreaded phone or doorbell ring when our to-do list outpaces our hours.

Dave Workman, President and co-founder of The Elemental Group

I have grown weary of seeing the weight of guilt laid on congregations by leaders who triumphantly declare unfailing victory over adversity. Andrew tells the story of his honest faith and like me, has found that sometimes we are left limping or worse from seasons in the desert. I share with him the belief that these are the very experiences that will position us where we can finally allow God to do a deep work in our souls.

Peter Holloway, Former Chief Executive Officer,
Prison Fellowship England & Wales

I'd just started reading Andrew's excellent new book on holy interruptions on the train when I received a text from a colleague asking me to galvanise prayer for an imminent fight. Cycling home from the station I wrestled with myself – should I fast as well as pray, having dreamt of my gin and tonic all the way home? In the end I fasted, many prayed and praise God she won a memorable victory. Andrew encourages us to see such interruptions as God-given opportunities. That's a mind shift that really shakes me out of my comfort zone. But his gentle challenge, personal stories and provocative questions are helping me ditch the irritation and seize the moment, with encouraging results!

Henrietta Blyth, Chief Executive Officer, Open Doors UK & Ireland

Andrew has created what all of us know we need, but often avoid: the opportunity to pause and reflect on our lives and our faith. I especially like the practical help at the end of each chapter which directs us in simple, accessible ways towards a better understanding of our own thought processes and patterns. The book is full of stories of his own and others' experience, which makes it a credible and entertaining read. I definitely felt a bit of an 'ouch' at times, which is probably a sign that his writing and insight is doing its job!

Steve Fenning, senior leader of the Forge Community

This book landed in my inbox on a typically busy day, and I must confess my immediate reaction to the interruption was, "No, not now"! This is despite my life having been (rudely) interrupted by a significant medical condition that needed surgical expertise, just this past year. It seems old habits die hard. With grace and wisdom this gem of a book helps us to alter our perception of life's interruptions and embrace the opportunity they can offer us of growth in the face of challenge. In an uncertain world where interruptions are increasingly inevitable and frequent, I commend this book to you, to accompany you on life's journey.

Alastair Bateman, Chief Executive Officer, Church Mission Society

In today's troubled world we daily hear of unexpected events which are often life changing for many people, and of course Covid-19 and the resultant lockdowns were major disruptors for all of us. In this excellent book Andrew encourages us to question whether such interruptions can actually be holy ones where God is trying to get our attention. If like me you prefer life to be much more predictable, then definitely read this book where interruptions are put into perspective, showing how we can make the most of even the worst of them. Worth interrupting your life to read!

Mervyn Thomas CMG, founder president, CSW

Life, Interrupted

Embracing God's invitations to change

Andrew Stewart-Darling

Foreword by Paul Harcourt

Authentic

Copyright © 2024 Andrew Stewart-Darling

30 29 28 27 26 25 24   7 6 5 4 3 2 1

First published 2024 by Authentic Media Limited,
PO Box 6326, Bletchley, Milton Keynes, MK1 9GG.
authenticmedia.co.uk
The right of Andrew Stewart-Darling to be identified as the Author of this Work
has been asserted in accordance with the
Copyright, Designs and Patents Act 1988.

All rights reserved.
No part of this publication may be reproduced, stored
in a retrieval system, or transmitted in any form or by any means,
electronic, mechanical, photocopying, recording or otherwise, without
the prior permission of the publisher or a licence permitting restricted
copying. In the UK such licences are issued by the Copyright Licensing
Agency, 5th Floor, Shackleton House, 4 Battle Bridge Lane, London SE1 2HX.

British Library Cataloguing in Publication Data
A catalogue record for this book is available from the British Library.
ISBN: 978-1-78893-344-5
978-1-78893-345-2 (e-book)

Unless otherwise marked, Scripture quotations are taken from
The Holy Bible, New International Version Anglicised
Copyright © 1979, 1984, 2011 Biblica
Used by permission of Hodder & Stoughton Ltd, an Hachette UK company.
All rights reserved.
'NIV' is a registered trademark of Biblica UK trademark number 1448790.

Scripture quotations marked CEV are from the Contemporary English Version
Copyright © 1991, 1992, 1995 by American Bible Society.
Used by Permission.

Scripture quotations marked KJV are from The Authorized (King James) Version.
Rights in the Authorized Version in the United Kingdom are vested in the Crown.
Reproduced by permission of the Crown's patentee, Cambridge University Press.

Scripture quotations marked MSG are from The Message, copyright © 1993,
2002, 2018 by Eugene H. Peterson. Used by permission of NavPress. All
rights reserved. Represented by Tyndale House Publishers.

Scripture quotations marked NLT are taken from the Holy Bible, New Living
Translation, copyright ©1996, 2004, 2015 by Tyndale House Foundation.
Used by permission of Tyndale House Publishers, Carol Stream, Illinois
60188. All rights reserved.

Cover design by Henry Milne
Printed and bound by CPI Group (UK) Ltd, Croydon, CR0 4YY

Dedication

*For Emma and my daughters: Daisy, Hattie and Matilda
who I am inclined to think make me the most blessed man on
God's earth.*

Contents

	Foreword	ix
	Introduction	1
1.	More than a Blip	11
2.	Things that Go Bump	19
3.	Stop Me if You Think You Have Heard This One Before	27
4.	Give Yourself a Break	41
5.	Use Your Imagination!	53
6.	How to be an Everyday Ordinary Hero	71
7.	May I Stop You Right There?	87
8.	To be Continued . . .	101
9.	Wet Feet	115
10.	You in the Future	127
11.	What Difference Does It Make?	139
12.	Intercession as Interruption	153
13.	Stir It Up!	163
14.	The Interruption of Rest	177

Epilogue	191
Acknowledgements	197
About the Author	199
Notes	200

Foreword

"

MAY YOU LIVE IN INTERESTING TIMES . . ."
ANCIENT CHINESE CURSE (APOCRYPHAL)

The times we live in are certainly interesting (in the sense of 'not normal'). They are strange. And they're often very disconcerting. I've lost count of the number of people who've said to me recently, 'I don't know what's going on anymore', 'I just don't know what'll happen next', 'I feel like I am not equipped for this', or something similar . . .

Many people feel as if they're having to run just to stand still. The old, familiar models of leadership don't work in this new world; political and economic models are undergoing tectonic shifts; institutions that have lasted centuries seem to be in trouble as never before. All of which mirrors the turbulence in our personal lives. A certain amount of unexpected and often, to us, undesirable change is normal in human experience. Nobody expects to sail through life without some disruption, but it seems that such unsettling moments are increasing in frequency.

In the first decade of this century, an acronym adopted by the US War College started to slip into more common parlance, first in business but later as a general description. 'VUCA' sums up the experience of the world we live in today – volatile, uncertain, complex and ambiguous. Things are volatile, meaning that they are unstable and subject to rapid change.

Foreword

Much is uncertain, where we simply don't have enough information to predict the outcome. No one would argue that the world is not becoming more complex. The incredible rise in the interconnectedness of things and the bewildering interactions of the systems that surround us mean that we often don't know what will happen when we change even one single thing. Finally, ambiguity expresses the lack of clarity with which we live, where what we do know doesn't seem to help us chart a confident course through the fog.

Is there going to be a 'new normal'? If there is one thing that I think we could confidently predict, it will be that our lives will increasingly experience interruptions, large and small. Those who learn to thrive are going to be those who not only learn to survive these changes, but who are able to learn from them. Not every interruption is a negative or challenging thing that we must deal with, but even those that are can be transformed into opportunities to discover more about ourselves, find fresh perspectives and treasure in life, and more of the God who loves us through every change and chance.

When you enter uncharted territory, it is helpful to have a guide. Andrew Stewart-Darling has had a career which spans the worlds of church and business, the charitable sector and marketing. In addition, he can draw on his own personal experiences. I know that he is a wise guide and an insightful mentor. Andrew's journey may have parallels to yours at some points, but – even when it doesn't – I am confident that his hard-won practical wisdom and his insights into the meaning of 'life in all of its fulness' will help you find greater joy in your own journey.

Paul Harcourt

Former national leader of New Wine,
vicar of All Saints' Woodford Wells

Introduction

" WE INTERRUPT THIS PROGRAMME..."

As I sit down to write . . .

An Amazon driver has knocked on the door.

Royal Mail have posted two letters, bringing crashing down with some force the internal letterbox draft excluder.

The family WhatsApp group has pinged four times.

The cat has come into the study and pestered me for food.

So if I can just have a minute to say . . . everyone please . . . quiet, I would like to tell you how I have come to this place today.

In January 2020 as I sharpened my pencil, or at least bought a new computer mouse, I began to outline the book you now hold in your hands. I knew where I wanted to go with it, but then something happened. Something unexpected.

It started with the news of an unknown virus in central China.

The World Health Organisation and chief medical experts came together to express their growing concern at the seriousness of its threat and officially categorised it as Corona Virus Disease 2019 – or Covid-19 for short.

By Wednesday 29 January 2020 the first case in the UK was recorded in York.

Panic ensued.

Within eight weeks the world experienced the biggest global upset since the Second World War. Our beautiful, small, blue planet would go into shut down. Life plans were consequently put on hold, along with this book which was now sounding more than just a little ironic.

I had thought once this pandemic had blown over after, say, six months, I would get back to what I did before – pastoring a church – but things weren't to turn out that way.

It was while trying to find ways to navigate the church through this extraordinary time that I became increasingly aware I was constantly exhausted. I had that kind of tiredness you don't recover from even after a few good nights' sleep.

With all the additional needs in the church I also realised in one week alone I had managed to clock up 71 hours.

As a bi-vocational church planting pastor, which contrary to opinion is not a neurological disorder, I was used to working two jobs. Before the pandemic I had been working, on average, a 55 to 60-hour week and had done so for some 14 years. It had become a normal way of life, but these extra hours were a whole new experience – and something was about to give.

Unknowingly, I had got the virus.

It turned into what became known months later as Long Covid. A hospital medic said in my instance it was likely I had got so sick because my immune system was shot due to long hours of work.

I was already struggling with poor mental health and, truth be known, suffering with burn-out, but I pushed on. After all, 'call is call' and, like other church leaders, I was keen to do as much as possible for our church and community. Besides, isn't this what leaders do in times of crises?

Early in the pandemic there was so much fear and paranoia around the word 'Coronavirus' that social media inevitably went into overdrive. Everyone seemed quick to dish out their folksy advice for protecting themselves. There was also a great deal of black humour and 'junk science' which was circulated quicker than free money. Vitamin B, paracetamol, hand sanitiser, flour and rice became precious commodities, along with toilet rolls. Although still no one can tell me why the last one was in such short supply.

During this uncertain time, I knew that a community church like ours had to continue to be a 'light on the hill' and find a way to keep its doors open when everyone else was being forced to shut theirs. And as the pastor I needed to lead from the front.

In the first half of 2020 not many people knew of someone directly who had this terrible virus. But I had my first suspicions I might have it when I was in our street clapping for the NHS on a Thursday night. I commented to a neighbour how my chest felt unusually tight.

THE NIGHT EVERYTHING CHANGED

I began to experience pain in my lungs, felt increasingly breathless and my whole body ached. When I lay down it felt as though someone had just placed an invisible baby elephant on my chest. There was no respite. No escape. Doing the simplest tasks felt like trying to walk up a mountain on roller-skates. At the time I just ploughed on, recognising we were living in unprecedented times – a phrase we would all come to overuse.

Eventually one night I was compelled to do a trip to Accident and Emergency but was told by a muffled voice behind several layers of personal protective gear that I would be at greater risk if I stayed in – so I was sent home. The initial symptoms, thankfully, were mostly manageable compared to the others I heard about. But it was the weeks and months to follow that would be the worst.

At that time my doctor candidly shared with me one afternoon that a few of his fellow patients had not made it. We sat in silence together for a few moments. I felt my heart become heavier but with a different kind of pain.

There was only one course of action. I simply had to stop to give myself a chance.

The chest pain, aching, breathlessness, fatigue, brain fog and other internal discomforts went on day after day, week after week, month after month with little change. It was unrelenting but it gave me an invaluable insight into what it was like living with a chronic illness, as some members of my church have had to do for so many years.

I spent a small fortune on vitamins, herbal remedies, prescribed medicines trying to find a way back to health, but very little had any effect.

Long Covid, as it later became known, began to have another consequence. It began to change the way I saw my spiritual life, my relationships, my identity, my understanding of work, my idea of progress and achievements. All the different strands of my life were coming together and being pulled into sharp focus.

It also caused me to reflect on my theology of healing and miracles. I mean, how much harder is it to find the courage to pray for someone with a long-term condition than with a sports injury or recent emotional setback?

It took me the best part of two years to recover and feel normal again. Although I still suffer today with some residual aching in my chest when I overdo it, but I thank God for my recovery – knowing other families are still grieving for their loss.

The pandemic virus has undoubtedly become the greatest interrupter to this generation, and we won't know fully the damage it has caused for still some time to come. It has impacted home life, the workplace, education, and how we now possibly socially connect with each other. It has also become the greatest interrupter to my life. But here's the thing: it has created the greatest opportunity to see the change I subconsciously wanted for myself.

Because the bottom line is, we all need to be interrupted more than we think.

In fact, I would go so far as to suggest that interruptions are vital. We might even want to call them holy disruptions – times and situations used by God to mercifully save us from unhealthy choices and unkind voices – not least the ones in our head.

I have been graciously forced on a journey to see that interruptions can have the power to restore hope, release faith, mend lives, heal memories and bring us closer to the heart of the Father.

In those months where I struggled to get enough air into my lungs, I cannot say I always coped well, and this so-called 'man of God' certainly did his fair share of complaining! There were times when I would panic when I couldn't catch my breath. I became anxious, fearful, but I was aware too that God's presence was never that far

Introduction 5

from me even when the next day felt like a week away. But I could find some peace knowing that God was continually at work in my health, and I saw over time how the Holy Spirit seemed to breathe in concert with each fight for breath.

I would pray for my daily bread – for air – to get me through each day. It was always enough but, like the manna in the desert, it was not something I could store. It kept me dependent on God and taught me that whatever happens, whatever interruptions lie ahead, his life in me will always be enough for any situation I would face.

God never holds his breath from us. As the writer of Job proclaims, 'The Spirit of God has made me; the breath of the Almighty gives me life.'[1]

FORCED INTERRUPTIONS

Now getting Covid-19 was a forced interruption, and you and I would understand this as meaning something that is outside of our control such as when someone unexpectedly knocks at the door just as you sit down to dinner. We can't plan for when it happens, which is why we end up getting frustrated and irritated by the situation. Of course, there are instances when we could just ignore it or pretend not to notice, but by this time it has already impacted us and forced us to act in one way or other.

But there is another side.

What if we are waiting for a knock at the door to give us the perfect excuse to leave the table without looking rude to our guests?

There are times when an interruption such as this or a phone call will change everything, much like in J.B. Priestley's famous 1945 play, *An Inspector Calls*, which sees a successful, upper middle-class family caught up in a moral blame game over the death of a known/unknown girl.

There will always be those interruptions that become disruptions and leave us in a state of turmoil and frustration. They will demand our full attention and may even call for a change of heart as with the Birling family and Gerald Croft in Priestley's play.

But it is what we do next that will define our character.

DISTRACTING OURSELVES

It might sound strange for a leader to say this, but I encourage my-self to be interrupted – and often in one of my favourite cafés. I will take a book or laptop with me knowing I might be stopped any time by someone passing by. In fact, I have moved from my desk in my study to a café as I write now, and know that it probably won't be long before I am forced to look up.

We may invite interruptions out of boredom or as a temporary es-cape from doing a stressful task, or when we need a distraction to give ourselves a rest. I can find myself easily arguing the positives and negatives for an interruption. Not least when trying to change the course of a conversation.

There is a scene in the war drama, *The Darkest Hour*, when Gary Oldman's Winston Churchill turns angrily to Lord Halifax and asks him to stop interrupting him even as Halifax is trying to interrupt Churchill.[2] It neatly sums up the problem of how we often communi-cate with each other. We do not always listen to hear but listen just enough to know when we can interrupt them with our own words. We will of course do it politely and respectfully but there are many times too when what is needed most from us is to say nothing and just be there with our kindness and understanding.

It seems only human to want to use an interruptive style to commu-nicate our thoughts and so we will happily spend much of our lives interrupting each other's interruptions because we have been condi-tioned to see it as the best way to be present and to be appreciated. But it can also backfire!

My wife, Emma, tells me that I often *abruptly* interrupt her or our daughters at the dinner table, which I am told sends out the signal that I am not valuing what is being said or, worse still, not listening because I am already distracted by something else and so I am only half in the conversation – which at times in all fairness is true.

But some interruptions cannot easily be brushed aside and leave us untouched, such as getting Covid-19, being made redundant from a long-term job, or a spouse deciding to leave us after twenty-five years. They will test something deeper in us and bring discomfort if not a searing pain with it.

DISCOVERING OUR LIMITS HELPS SAVE US

If we can be truly honest with ourselves, we tend to see the interruptions we make as the ways and means to control a situation to get the outcome we want to see.

To not be able to interrupt someone or a situation will always feel like a loss of power, which is uncomfortable and can leave us feeling anxious. It is within this raw moment of revelation that we are forced to confront our own limitations. We realise we are not in control as much as we would like to be. We are simply creatures, not the Creator.

John the Baptist knew this well when his followers became upset that the crowds were leaving him to follow Jesus. He responded as a man who knew how to live within his limits and said, 'A person can receive only what is given them from heaven.'[3]

Confronting the myth that everything can stay the same in our control, given the right space and circumstances, is not only unhelpful but actually harmful to the view we have of ourselves. It is the very sacrifice of self-empowerment and the desire to control outcomes that will see us gain in more ways than we can possibly imagine for ourselves. It will in fact have a power to grow us closer to Jesus Christ to become wholly one in him. As Peter Scazzero says, 'Embracing our limits humbles us like little else.'[4]

I INTERRUPT, THEREFORE I AM

I have found that embracing my own limits gives me a reality to work with that helps me see that I don't need to make myself feel special by being successful at life through achievements.

Knowing our own limitations, which I have found are never fixed but only flex more with age and circumstance, can have a profound effect on our desire for contentment and overall happiness. But it is in those 'still moments' when I happen to stumble into the presence of Jesus, away from this exhausting pursuit of idolising a successful life, that I realise how much my soul wants to seek less of the world and more of him. I am liberated from seeking importance through performance to become a child of God again.

Here is something else to be aware of. Living within our limits also means there is always work for the Holy Spirit to do in addressing the problem of our 'true self' versus our 'false self', two terms coined by psychoanalyst Donald Winnicott. For instance, how do we know when we have found our real spiritual self? What does it look like? When do we know when we have an authentic self? I'll give you a clue here . . . it is to do with peace and contentment.

One thing I can say for sure is do not expect a thunderbolt of revelation! It is likely to come as a gradual realisation as you grow more in faith. Look for small signs of dissatisfaction with a life being built on achievements, acknowledgements and needing to be special. Allow yourself to be pruned and ask God to put a desire in you that wants to strive less and live more through the presence of Jesus in you.

As you go through this book, don't be surprised if the Holy Spirit offends your mind to expose your heart or gives you a holy nudge to repent for things that you may have always seen as okay distractions. As with John the Baptist, it is about how we embrace the surrendering of our limitations that will help set us up for what comes next.

Okay so before we move on, I would like to invite you to pray and begin to acknowledge how there may just be a need in you to control outcomes and how it could be subconsciously informing your reactions to interruptions and how you are choosing to interrupt others. Because here is the thing, and it is a big thing, it may just be that how you respond is causing more pain than you know. The good news, it can begin to change today.

Take a moment now to stop, breathe, maybe silently count to ten, and invite God to step into your thoughts, then I might suggest praying this prayer out loud. Pause for a minute or two afterwards and then we will turn the page and look at how a rookie sea captain out of his depth deals with the interruption of rain.

INTERRUPTER

A PRAYER OF SURRENDER

Heavenly Father,

I bring you my desire to surrender.

To relearn how to be attentive, present, and open,
Knowing too it could fully undo me.

But I will trust in your goodness and gentlest of ways,
even when everything in me shouts 'resistance!'

I so much want to be the one in control.

I so want to be the CEO of my own future.

Yet, today, I choose to make myself small,
to silence my thoughts to hear you say:

'Come, let me lead the way, see where I take you.
Experience my yoke and walk with me.'

So I invite you, Holy Spirit, to bring your interruptions.

Break in and draw me ever closer to the one who loves me unwaveringly.

Unreservedly. Unequivocally. Unendingly.

Amen.

1 MORE THAN A BLIP

At first, we treated Covid-19 as a blip, much in the same way that rain stops play at Lord's Cricket Ground on a warm summer's day. It was inconvenient and frustrating, but at this point the numbers of those dying were still relatively low. Many of us chose to deal with it by taking it all in our stride.

Remember, at this time no one was wearing a mask – we were simply washing our hands a lot and using hand sanitiser to the tune of 'Happy Birthday' when we could get it. It was just something to get through until the sun shone through the small black clouds again and we could pick up where we left off.

This attitude tends to be our normal default response to anything that interrupts us. There seems to be an in-built switch in our heads that likes to believe that, given a bit of time, things will go back to as they were before. Blind optimism perhaps, but it is often a response fuelled by wishful thinking more than faith or a close knowledge of the situation.

But there comes a point when an interruption becomes too prolonged and needs to be upgraded to the status of *disruption*.

The pandemic, of course, became more than a temporary stoppage. At first it was like an amber traffic light before turning to red. We believed it would soon change to green but instead it turned to red, leading us to eventually 'turn off the engine', to sit in the silence with others, wondering when our lives would begin moving again.

"
TO LOOK ASLAN IN THE EYES WE NEED COURAGE FROM HIS GRACE."
BROTHER BERNARD[1]

"
LET US THEN APPROACH GOD'S THRONE OF GRACE WITH CONFIDENCE, SO THAT WE MAY RECEIVE MERCY AND FIND GRACE TO HELP US IN OUR TIME OF NEED."
HEBREWS 4:16

I was affected in another way that I could not have imagined. I remember one particular day when I was told by the doctor that I was now classified as someone with a chronic illness. Apparently, anyone who is seriously ill for over six weeks falls into this category. I was stunned to pick up this new label.

I asked God if this was the 'new normal' for my life. At the time I felt my question was met with silence. There was also scant medical encouragement as so little was known about the virus back then.

Meanwhile, we took advantage of the glorious summer weather at home. Not many of my neighbours complained about being unable to commute into work or having to find a way to work from home. Even our pets seemed happier; dogs saw more of their owners and enjoyed longer walks than usual.

As time went on, doubts began to emerge that life would go back to normal after August, as had been first suggested. Meantime, we had all dutifully followed the government's advice, stayed distant from each other, worn masks, queued two metres apart at the supermarket and made the most of our allowed daily walk – some with newly acquired puppies.

With the grim weekly updates of numbers of those dying from Covid-19, we slowly turned from being breezy optimists into paranoid neighbours. We became fearful of each other and increasingly confused with what was the right thing to do. Even all this time later, sociologists and educationalists still believe it will be some time before we know just how much damage the pandemic has done to the fabric of our society.

Disruptions, by their nature, don't just break up a situation, they break something inside of us. Looking back, we can see how the world became traumatised by the sheer loss of life and how people grieved the loss of control over their future. This is something sadly that others still must live with daily, such as those thousands of broken, hurting families in the Ukraine who are 'just existing' in a constant state of uncertainty and anxiety.

And this is the problem with trauma, which is a condition brought on through times of abnormal stress, a Greek word that, in its simplest form, means 'wound'. But it is more than a wound as the root word *teirein* means something that rubs away at us. It has the power to

More than a Blip 13

twist and bore its way into our emotional state, to pierce our heart, leaving us feeling hopeless.

We find this word used to great effect in Jesus' parable of the Good Samaritan. The Jewish traveller was not only severely beaten and left to die but also rejected by his own people – twice. The third person to come along was a hated outsider to the Jewish community, who you would rightly think meant that the attacked man was undeserving of his kindness, yet unexpectedly the stranger chooses to see the stricken traveller. But he does so much more.

He addresses the whole person: the pain of being mugged and the pain of rejection. Doctor Luke, the gospel writer, describes how the compassionate Samaritan tends to the wounded man with such generosity, and with the one simple aim of bringing him back to physical, emotional and spiritual health. 'He went to him and band-aged his wounds [trauma], pouring on oil and wine. Then he put the man on his own donkey, brought him to an inn and took care of him.'[2]

A MATTER OF PERSPECTIVE

On my old commuter line into Liverpool Street station, an interruption to a train service was shown on the board as a 'delay', of which there were many, but when there were damaged overhead power cables it was upgraded as a 'disruption'.

So what if an interruption – or disruption – is just a matter of perspective?

After all, trains will probably run again the next day according to the set timetable. Yesterday's delayed train will just be something in the past that is quickly forgotten.

A real disruption means there would be no quick return to the sched-uled times of trains, but good can also come out of these times – it is just putting ourselves in a place to be able to see it.

There are many times in the Bible when God chooses to break into a life and stop it in its tracks to bring a change of direction. And in the Old Testament it probably doesn't come much bigger than the story of the Great Flood.

THE TALE OF AN ANCIENT MARINER

> Now the earth was corrupt in God's sight and was full of violence. God saw how corrupt the earth had become, for all the people on earth had corrupted their ways. So God said to Noah, 'I am going to put an end to all people, for the earth is filled with violence because of them. I am surely going to destroy both them and the earth.
>
> *Genesis 6:11–13*

God declares that he is going to bring disruption to the corruption and start the world again.

So before his six-hundredth birthday God tells Noah to build an ark because heavy rain is due. Now a massive building project is probably the last thing you need when you are getting on in years, but Noah and his family were picked out by God because of his righteousness. They were given a ticket out of a corrupt society that had become immoral, violent and completely out of control.[3]

Newly made Captain Noah sets about building the ark, which is to be made from cypress wood, based on the maker's instructions.

Now here's the interesting thing: after reading these instructions in some detail I can find no mention in Genesis of how to sail it. Something that would be alarming for any captain to find out! But maybe that should not be so surprising as we often assume the ark was boat-shaped through reading old Sunday-school stories.

There is simply no mention of sails or how to navigate the waters. It was just expected to float on the water like a big wooden box, which is actually what the word 'ark' means, coming from the Latin *arca*, the term for a chest or box. It meant Noah and his family were totally in God's hands in the global crisis and had to go wherever the stormy waters took them.

Most church leaders, if being honest, will tell you how much they struggle with not being in control and find it a challenge to be truly led by the Holy Spirit. The thought of 'letting go and letting God' is far from easy when faced with a situation where they have no say – such as being caught up in a pandemic lockdown where normal church services can't resume.

Emma, my wife and co-pastor, and I felt like this for most of the pandemic. We had little control on how to steer the church through it, beyond keeping it afloat like a big box, but it became a place of safety.

More than a Blip 15

It also became a place of close community, prayer and compassion for one another with WhatsApp groups, prayer texts, Zoom gatherings, telephone calls, online services, along with Online Alpha, and children and youth ministries. We also managed to keep our food-bank open every week thanks to our amazingly dedicated team. We might not have had control where we were going as a church but, by the grace of God, we managed to stay buoyant in a time when the pandemic threatened many millions of lives and livelihoods.

We know from Genesis that for a while the rescue package worked. After the waters receded and the earth began to be repopulated, the descendants of Noah were blessed and flourished under their renewed covenant with God.

But we all know what happened next. After a while the plan to end all evil began to fail because clever old humankind learnt how to sin again, which brought with it new pain, chaos and sorrow.

However, God was never wrong-footed and always knew the ark had its limitations, which we now understand was a foreshadow of what was to later come out of Nazareth many centuries later. As the writer of Hebrews said: 'By faith Noah, when warned about things not yet seen, in holy fear built an ark to save his family. By his faith he condemned the world and became heir of the righteousness that is in keeping with faith.'[4]

Take a quick flick through your Bible and you'll see one person after another having their life continually interrupted by a faithful, patient, loving and kind God. We see righteous people being interrupted, such as Noah and Abraham, as well as sinful people being interrupted, such as Matthew and Paul. But all through the book God mercifully speaks into the hearts and minds of ordinary people to reset the whole course of human history to restore the relationship with him. Something wonderful emerges that is permanent, eternal and unbreakable.

It becomes overwhelmingly clear through Scripture that it was always God's intention to interrupt our lives with acts of love and break into our brokenness to Save Our Souls.

The Creator of heaven and earth does not stay distant like a non-plussed Greek deity but gets involved in the everyday sweat and toil of the human experience. And later, we will look at the greatest disruption of all in human history, the most permanent and immutable action ever taken to change the course of the world – once and for all.

16 *Life, Interrupted*

Meanwhile, we can say with some confidence that forced interruptions are not something that we will naturally welcome or even want to celebrate – not unless we can see they have clear merit.

SAVED BY THE BELL!

There are times when you may have heard a fire alarm and been told to quickly stop what you are doing, exit the building and meet at an outside assembly point.

I guarantee that we will see that as a distraction from what we are doing. We may even mutter our frustration under our breath for not being able to finish something, but the bell rings for the sole purpose of saving our life. That bell is a reminder that our life is incredibly valuable – and not just to the boss!

It is only when we see smoke billowing into the sky with red flames licking up the sides of the building that our irritation turns to gratitude.

But let me paint another less dramatic scenario.

It is a quiet start to my Saturday morning. It is my one day off in the week. I am making a cooked breakfast while listening to a 'slow Saturday' playlist on my smart speaker. Then, out of nowhere, one of my daughters comes in and decides to make a kale, cucumber, blueberry with cacao – or whatever-it-is – smoothie. It can't wait. It must be done right this instant.

I huff and puff and without using words make it known that I am put out. The blender is not quiet, which makes it hard for me to listen to the speaker, but still my daughter continues undaunted in her task.

'There, done,' she says and slides one of the two glasses over to me. 'Here you go, Dad!'

I cannot but confess feelings of both shame and appreciation. I am humbled, but I am also grateful. It is not what I had planned, but I concede the smoothie is healthy and not unpleasant on the taste buds. In fact, I am up for a refill.

This is often the tension we feel when God interrupts us. We love God and love his ways, but sometimes they seem to be at odds with our own plans and, let's face it, at times irritating and inconvenient. At no point does the interruption look kind or remotely helpful. It is underappreciated and certainly doesn't always have our full attention, but when we taste God's goodness, wow! Something changes in us.

C.S. Lewis said, 'The great thing, if one can, is to stop regarding all the unpleasant things as interruptions of one's "own," or "real" life. The truth is of course that what one calls the interruptions are precisely one's real life – the life God is sending one day by day.'[5]

Jesus was the expert in interruptions and could easily change the course of a conversation with a deft word or two. He would choose to constantly interrupt the Pharisees and scribes with his own interpretation of the Torah by using a story or illustration. Sometimes Jesus would underline it with a miracle or sign, but it never failed to get their attention. He also knew he was not breaking into something that was not already broken and needing to be fixed.

INTERVENTIONS

Interruptions are the interventions that change us. They are the obtrusions God will use to offend our minds to expose our true heart's condition, to stop a growing catalogue of foolish mistakes and poor choices – but always with a purpose to renew life, along with a chance to become who we were always meant to be.

So here's the thing: what if we could be more open, trusting and welcoming to the interventions of God?

What if these times could save or improve our marriages and other relationships and begin to mend trust, restore broken dreams, and save us from damaging ourselves and the ones we love? These kinds of interruptions that are full of grace because they give us another chance to recalibrate our thinking and come to our senses.

Now if the only way God can get us to look up from what we are doing is to interrupt us, would we really begrudge him from stopping us doing the thing we are doing in that moment? And knowing how hard it is to stop ourselves, wouldn't we feel just a little bit relieved too? Not least because sin is enjoyable, and we know it is going to need an external perspective to change our mindset.

So here's a prayer of attention to say before we continue. You might want to read it through first before praying it. Take your time in saying each line, making spaces to pause. Allow the Holy Spirit to inhabit a phrase or highlight a word to you. Remember, prayer is a dialogue, not a monologue. It is a conversation between two people who love each other.

INTERRUPTER

A PRAYER TO ALLOW INTERRUPTIONS TO CHANGE US

Heavenly Father, I rejoice that I always have your fullest attention. Thank you for placing my head close to my heart to enable me to worship you intimately in truth and spirit.

Lord Jesus, you have loved me before I could love you, myself or my neighbour. Help me to accept all that I am, to be all I can be, through all that you are in me.

Holy Spirit, where I have no control or no say, help me to still see each interruption as an invitation to change. When they humiliate me, change me. When they break me, humble me. May I always have ears to listen, a mind to understand, and a heart to respond.

Amen.

2 THINGS THAT GO BUMP!

I'd love to say that I always loved learning but that would simply not be true. So it will come as no surprise that I didn't particularly like school very much, and hardly excelled, which made it even more remarkable that I still managed to stumble my way into a place of higher education. As the poet John Pomfret remarked, 'We live and learn, but not the wiser grow.'[2] That felt like me. However, perspective is everything.

The only way of learning from personal experiences is to reflect on them, something that Emperor Julius Caesar had done and took the selfless time to write down for us, which he said later attributed to him seeing even greater success.[3]

But after time at school, along with the additional years of further and higher education, I felt I had got what I needed. I had figured out where I wanted to work, where I wanted to live, the kind of person I wanted to be – and even the kind of family I wanted to have.

I was unstoppable in my ambitions, if a little lazy, more of a steam-roller on steroids than an athlete on adrenaline. If Lewis Carroll's Queen of Hearts 'believed six impossible things before breakfast', I was pretty sure I could give her a good run for her money.[4] Being blessed with a creative brain I was buzzing with no end of ideas and really didn't see the need to stop for too long to see if my decisions were right or not.

All this wonderful youthful thinking was set on the backdrop of the 1980s: a time of tall hair, padded shoulders and ridiculously baggy T-shirts.

"

YOU WILL NOT SLEEP, IF YOU LIE THERE A THOUSAND YEARS, UNTIL YOU HAVE OPENED YOUR HAND AND YIELDED THAT WHICH IS NOT YOURS TO GIVE OR TO WITHHOLD. YOU MAY THINK YOU ARE DEAD, BUT IT WILL BE ONLY A DREAM; YOU MAY THINK YOU HAVE COME AWAKE, BUT IT WILL STILL BE ONLY A DREAM. OPEN YOUR HAND, AND YOU WILL SLEEP INDEED – THEN WAKE INDEED."
GEORGE MACDONALD[1]

> **"WAKE UP! STRENGTHEN WHAT REMAINS AND IS ABOUT TO DIE."**
> REVELATION 3:2

This was the era when we thought non-stop disco remixes were a good idea. You may not care to remember, or hopefully are too young to know, but Jive Bunny, an invention of a DJ from Rotherham, struck upon the idea of sampling lots of well-known songs and putting them altogether into one long mega track. They took out all the breaks and pauses between hits and set them all at the same tempo with a backbeat. This was all about keeping the party going on the dance floor.

And, wow, were they irritating! It was like having a five-course meal served on the same plate and using the same spoon for everything. It became a metaphor for the non-stop noise of the constant busyness in my head.

Maybe though this is a common experience for many of us. We hope that, if we are not forced to stop, we will be able to dance our way through any situation or crisis. Our mantra becomes one of just keep moving and everything will be okay.

We will take what we believe to be good and true, create a narrative of comfort around it, and then defend it furiously. This was certainly the Red Queen's logic until challenged by a curious seven-and-a-half-year-old girl called Alice.

Whether it is arrogance or not there are likely to be various non-stop conversations we have with ourselves about the way our life should go. We may not be sure where they will finish, but we know they don't allow for any upsets. Ambition doesn't know how to.

For instance, on my social media feed I read how a church leader publicly confessed that he had not given himself a Sunday off for nearly three years. He admitted it was not good, but then somehow managed to turn it into a badge of honour, and so said he would keep going. It shows an unhealthy propensity that even on our most tired and poorly judged days we can't help but need to stroke our own ego and seek approval from someone.

PUSHING DOORS

It is not hard to see how we can harbour a deep anxiety with the thought of stopping and for the most obvious of reasons – it simply isn't in our game plan. There is little or no contingency made for taking

Things that Go Bump! 21

a pause because so much of what we do is performance-driven by our need to see continual success. Interruptions are mostly seen as annoyances.

At the heart of it is the f-word.

Fear.

We fear a forced stop. We fear it won't allow us to pick up where we left off. And that frightens us because we are scared it will throw our carefully cultivated plans into a place of doubt and the unknown.

Fear paralyses us. It is the opposite feeling to those times when we have an emotional high brought on by certitude or conviction. These may be the times when we think we should be wearing an obvious cloak of humility and dialling it down to be more acceptable, even though the confidence and rising hope in us could be something gifted in that moment by the Holy Spirit.

The poet, writer and social activist, William Morris, observed about himself, 'I determined to do no less than to transform the world with Beauty. If I have succeeded in some small way, if only in one small corner of the world, amongst the men and women I love, then I shall count myself blessed, and blessed, and blessed, and the work goes on.'[5]

Uninterrupted vision and determination are powerful allies.

But there is always a fear that the vision we have for ourselves will never be fully realised. The fear of being stopped holds us hostage and at worst cripples us, making us increasingly anxious with every unplanned upset. It has the power to keep us feeling fragile and fearful of the future.

We always hope that God is on our side to help us push through, so we utilise in our prayer the words of Jesus: 'Ask and it will be given to you; seek and you will find; knock and the door will be opened to you.'[6]

Without being aware of it we are praying a prayer for 'unstoppability', not for compatibility with God's will. We want the doors to stay open no matter what, so we say our performance-driven 'open sesame' prayer to help us keep pushing through with our self-made desires.

There is a desperation in us that this approach somehow will bring Jesus around to our way of thinking, all so we don't have to have the inconvenience or disappointment of having to change our thinking. I wonder though at times if this approach has more to do with self-entitlement. I mean, who hasn't prayed, 'I am doing this for you, Lord, so will you do this for me!'? Signed, 'Your humble servant'.

The words of Jesus in Matthew's Gospel are an invitation for a relationship, not the words of a genie in a bottle who grants three wishes. To want to 'ask, seek and knock' are meant to be the actions of a person with a desire to receive with gratitude whatever gifts Jesus puts in our hands. The power of these words is amplified in the last book of the Bible in the revelation to John seen and understood as encouragement to the church in Philadelphia; 'What he opens no one can shut, and what he shuts no one can open. I know your deeds. See, I have placed before you an open door that no one can shut.'[7]

The only things I can see that God wants us to keep doing uninterruptedly is to keep drawing closer to him, to keep loving him, to keep surrendering to him, to keep loving others and not give up when we are knocked back.

To 'ask, seek and knock' are the loving instructions that stand in the doorway to lead us into his holy presence to bring meaning to those deepest desires in us, which actually emanate from God, but were anonymous until revealed to us. Those things that we had strongly wanted to keep moving forward, no matter what, get replaced with an even stronger desire to rest in his presence. As Jacob exclaimed, and we can echo, 'How awesome is this place! This is none other than the house of God; this is the gate of heaven.'[8]

IT'S TOUGH TO FEEL YOU'RE NOT ENOUGH

You may be someone with leadership responsibilities in a church or an organisation where you feel there's an expectation for your faith and relationship with God to always be solid. But inside there is a growing uneasiness. Something is gnawing away that is affecting your confidence. And it has been there for some time. You tell yourself that you are not all you could be. You feel by now you should be better than you are. And worst of all, it makes you feel a fraud and a failure. It is your Achilles' heel, your one big weak spot.

Now have you noticed how easily the enemy seems to find this pressure point every single time you sit down to study, stand up to speak or stand in the company of your peers?

These fears and anxieties are as old as a stuttering Moses and as common as the cold but, like a cold, it is surprising how much we are willing to spend on this condition to keep us going – rather than just do the sensible thing and . . . stop and rest to recover.

You might write yourself a prescription to attend another church, go to another conference, seek another prayer course, buy another book, subscribe to another podcast – if a leader, take another sabbatical – but none of these things, however worthy, will be enough to break a habit that leaves you feeling six inches shorter than you should be.

We realise this fear is a negative thought pattern and getting help would be a good idea, but because we are busy there just doesn't ever feel as though there is a right time to unlearn wrong thoughts. But here's the reality: left unchecked, it will lead to some kind of burn-out.

Because you and I know there is an unsaid pressure on us that says there is never a good time to get sick, sad or exhausted. So we tend to lock our true thoughts and feelings away for the simple reason that even the predictability of unhealthy patterns has its comforts. But there is often confusion in what passes as comfort. It can also be an addiction.

It is a badly kept secret that anxiety disorder is on the increase everywhere. A global survey carried out by Gallup World Poll showed that one in three people, around two billion adults, reported signs of poor mental wellbeing.[9] It has been called a 'globalisation of emotion.' The world is being united in a different way – through sadness, worry and anger.

We absorb this information as much as the caffeine in our coffee while holding onto the hope of the cross and the power of the resurrection. But at times it can feel those things that make us fearful are just plain relentless, unsparing, assaulting our senses with no regard to whether they find us in a good place or not.

SWITCHING OFF

I am just old enough to remember when the BBC used to finish their transmissions each night by playing the National Anthem. It feels quaint to think of it nowadays, but in some way it said to us, maybe subconsciously, that everything is going to be all right as we finish this day.

Hearing an anthem that upholds the idea of a monarchy blessed and overseen by God reminded us all of the assurance of a higher power constantly reigning over us. Also, of course, it was time to go to bed because you had to go work the next day.

How this experience seems to contrast with today's streaming services such as Netflix and Prime where there is no end of content and

24   *Life, Interrupted*

no pronounced 'full stop' to mark the finish of one day before starting another. Nothing concludes. Everything is designed to keep us alert, engaged and seeking more.

Take the 'Big Apple'. As much as I love New York I find its nickname, 'the city that never sleeps', just a little bit exhausting and intimidating. It is meant to conjure up the excitement of living in a vibrant city, a place where there is always something going on, night and day. But it seems there is a price to pay for this.

Only one in four New Yorkers get the recommended eight hours' sleep a night – with half of them getting no more than six hours of shut-eye. They lead busy city lives but will spend their day worrying about material things like money and possessions. There are constant internal conversations going on of 'Do I have enough? Can I make my bills? Am I putting enough away?'[10]

Michael Jackson sang, 'Don't stop 'til you get enough.' And this is the problem as we are being constantly bombarded with this message all the time. It can't help but generate a fear of never having enough of anything – at least for too long.

EPISODES

Our day's activities can be seen as 'episodes', such as sleep, time with God, showering, cleaning teeth, driving to work, being at work, driving home, dinner, home group, TV and night-time routine.

We will allocate time to each episode to help us schedule our day and be able to move from one episode to the next with ease. Think of it like the BBC without commercial breaks.

The problem is, thanks to multitasking with technology, we are now adding far more episodes to our day than ever before. Every time the phone interrupts us, a new episode is being added. Jenevieve Treadwell sends a stark warning of the consequences of an ever-increasingly jam-packed schedule: 'Interruptions may seem small but they add up. This is called time confetti. You have an hour for exercise but this is broken up by taking a call or letting out the cat. This hour now feels more compressed and leads to people feeling like time is getting away from them.'[11] Left unattended it will leave us increasingly overwhelmed and constantly tired, with no clear boundaries for ourselves.

Something needs to interrupt us and how our brains have learnt, rather effectively, to spend our hours lurching from one episode to another, worrying, making decisions on the spot, and living with a countdown clock that tells us each birthday that we only have a limited time left to make it on God's green earth – and all this begins to say to us that our life purpose comes only through being continually productive.

But if we were to pause for just a moment and consider the world and the universe – which is poetically described in Genesis as being made in six days, not six minutes – it might give us an insight into how to live our lives with a different set of values.

Have you ever noticed how the first chapter of the first book of the Bible closes the account of creation with an exuberant celebration? And it is only said when finally, humankind is made, which seems to be what all the other days before are leading up to: 'God saw all that he had made, and it was very good. And there was evening, and there was morning.'[12] It is a wonderful picture that captures God's complete enthusiasm for us. And did you notice it has the word *very* thrown in there?

But if we get out of this verse and chapter only God's amazingly high levels of productivity in a short time, we will have missed the point, because this is how the story of creation begins to direct us to the words Jesus would say many centuries later: 'For God *so loved the world* that he gave his one and only Son, that whoever believes in him shall not perish but have eternal life.'[13]

Psychologists seem very clear of the consequences if we leave our emotional state of health unchecked when continually seeking more. It could mean a lifetime of fear stuck in a self-perpetuating cycle of defeat and frustration.

So it is important to notice the second part of the verse in Genesis, which speaks of night and day not as rivals to each other, but as symbols of God's continuous creative movement in our lives. They are an encouragement to us of his presence in and around us and not reminders that we have to be 'productive' with each day before the sun goes down, and perhaps to destroy any myth we have of ourselves that if we haven't been productive, we have somehow failed ourselves and God.

This all helps to see how we can overcome our never being enough or doing enough with the time and resources at our disposal. So before we move on, let's take a moment to do a quick health check.

INTERRUPTER

ARE YOU A DIGITAL FIDGET?

1. When you get up in the morning what is your daily regime?

    a. Open your Bible and pray (book or phone version)
    b. Read your texts and WhatsApp messages and then open your Bible and pray
    c. Read your newsfeed, texts and WhatsApp messages and then open your Bible and pray
    d. Read your social media feeds, newsfeed, texts, WhatsApp messages and then open your Bible and pray
    e. None of the above because I manage to live like a monk akin to the desert fathers and mothers of old. My whole day is filled with God's word and prayer. I am never interrupted. God is good!

2. As you come into a place of prayer how long is it before you get an urge to check messages and social media feeds?

    a. 1 minute
    b. 10 minutes
    c. 1 hour
    d. Longer

3. When you sit down for a meal, can you leave your phone in your pocket or on silent in another room without having a second thought?

4. What is the longest time, on average, you have gone without checking your phone?

    a. 15 minutes or less
    b. 1 hour
    c. A day
    d. A week
    e. 30 days and longer

5. How are you feeling about yourself right now?

Don't fret, I struggle too. We are in this together.

3 STOP ME IF YOU THINK YOU HAVE HEARD THIS ONE BEFORE

How did you score?

Much has been written about the darkening effect on the soul of non-stop digital content, no less so than the effect it has on our mental health, but it doesn't mean we have to now stop talking about it. Otherwise, the enemy wins, right? The cycle needs to be broken somewhere.

For instance, when I continually check my phone, I am aware it steals my time and draws my attention away from other people. It is not simply about a fear of missing out, it is about the endless opportunities it promises. And we all know we have got too attached to our devices when we can't go to sleep at night without one last check before turning off the lights. Ever wondered why we do it?

We might have started scrolling earlier as a distraction, out of boredom, or something to occupy our mind while we stand in a queue, but then something else starts to kick in. Psychologists call this operant conditioning.

This is where the mind learns through the consequences of doing something that it can be rewarded, which makes it want to do it again and again. We find one funny meme and then we want to find another.

> **THERE ARE SO MANY THINGS TO SAY, OF COURSE. ONE THING IS THAT WHETHER ONE LIFE IS ENOUGH OR NOT ENOUGH, ONE LIFE IS ALL WE GET, AT LEAST ONLY ONE LIFE HERE, ONLY ONE LIFE IN THIS GORGEOUS AND HAIR-RAISING WORLD, ONLY ONE LIFE WITH THE RANGE OF POSSIBILITIES FOR DOING AND BEING THAT ARE OPEN TO US NOW."**
>
> FREDERICK BUECHNER[1]

> **"THE THIEF COMES ONLY TO STEAL AND KILL AND DESTROY; I HAVE COME THAT THEY MAY HAVE LIFE, AND HAVE IT TO THE FULL."**
> JESUS[2]

It is why we find it so hard to stop because every reward gives a boost to the pleasure centres of the brain to keep reinforcing that behaviour in us. All the time our mind is being further removed from living in the present and missing out on meaningful moments happening around us.

But there are signs that we are waking up to the problem and taking seriously the triggers to this addictive behaviour. John Mark Comer, the former pastor of Bridgetown Church and author, is widely known for his forty-day fasts from social media during the time of Lent. He has understood that a harmless habit is, perhaps, not so harmless that it won't bring a disruption to his interior life.

I am not suggesting digital content is an enemy but all the time we scroll it always has the danger to rob us of something infinitely better, such as being aware of God in and around us.

We can become obsessed with online news and views, which we all know have the power to leave us judgemental, negative and fearful. Not finding a way to protect our mind will lead only to our general unhappiness and detachment from the gift of real-life relationships.

ADDICTS FOR SMART LIVING

Unless we can find a way to reduce the influences on our brain our soul will continue to suffer and feel abandoned.

There was a movement among Christians in the 1990s, mostly in America, where bracelets were worn which said 'WWJD', meaning 'What would Jesus do?' It feels now it is more of a case of 'What does Google say I should do?' Now the fact that nine out of ten people own a smartphone makes it a universal problem.

The average person spends 4.8 hours a day on their device. That equates to one third of the working day.[3] We have unknowingly become addicts and grown dependent on technology for our satisfaction, but we are also addicts for quick wisdom which is probably why 'life hacks' often come up in searches.

Stop Me if You Think You Have Heard This One Before   29

It all begs the question: How comfortable are we with having how we think and feel curated through one source?

For centuries there was only one other source and that was the Bible – of course, once it had been translated into a common language beyond Latin and made available to all!

Not many people are so sorted that they can find all the answers within themselves, which is why we have become friends with search engines and voice-controlled personal assistants. But what if we decide to interrupt the free flow of search content?

What if we could find a way to live as God always intended? What if we could live an unvarnished, transparent life, free to be ourselves in every way – a place of no negativity or fear where we can live through Christ, in Christ and with Christ?

This is the gift interruptions give us. A place to stop to be grateful with what we have already received rather than continually chasing rewards, thinking enough is never enough.

When we take the time to re-centre on Jesus and become still, our soul can relax and find its rest, which then is an encouragement to our mind to stop searching elsewhere for its happiness.

It has been said that the only creature that resists being itself is us, humankind. Think about that for a moment because this is important – when we resist God, we are at the same time resisting joy and our complete emotional and spiritual wellbeing.

It should come as no great surprise that when our minds are flooded with external information our desire for God becomes less. And when our trust in his ways becomes dimmed, we can easily turn and 'ask, seek and knock' on the door of the internet to look for a quick hit of hope and an instant dose of happiness.

So here is some good news for you and it comes in the form of a prayer of King David: 'Search me, God, and know my heart; test me and know my anxious thoughts. See if there is any offensive way in me, and lead me in the way everlasting.'[4]

Stop striving and thinking you are not like everybody else and accept that you are. Stop surrendering to endless information and start surrendering to an infinite God who has your joy at the centre of his intentions for you.

YOUR 'GO TO'

In my experience, searching for a breakthrough is seldom an isolated or solitary spiritual discipline. To interrupt the cycle I can think of no better starting point than turning to a Jesus-centred trusted circle of friends.

Dietrich Bonhoeffer suggested that the best way to get yourself interrupted is to intentionally put interrupters around you. 'Let the person who cannot be alone beware of community. Let the person who is not in community beware of being alone.'[5] We may feel alone with our needs and issues, but it is the gift of community that knows and cares for each other that helps to see the change we long to see for ourselves.

We need to be in situations where someone says to us, 'I hear what you are saying; can I share something that might help you?' or 'What do you mean by "ABC"?' or 'Before you move on, I remember last week you said you would do "XYZ". Just wondered how it went?'

Over the years I have learnt that a small gathering like a midweek home group is a place to be interrupted, and often. But the group works best if everyone comes as an interrupter and is willing to make themselves vulnerable – and that can only happen when a pattern of trust is formed through shared stories and experiences. Little by little our thought patterns will begin to change and our lives will start to be governed by a different narrative. That midweek interruption will help us to believe that we have more to gain by stopping and listening to trusted voices than keeping going and hoping for the best.

John Wimber, founder of the Vineyard Church movement, always said that the best small groups are when people are real with God and real with one another. This has certainly been my experience. They are often unexpected places of holy ground where we will cry and celebrate with each other in equal measure.

WHEN LIFE BUMPS YOU

Meantime we can take it as read that something will always come along and try and knock us off our perch. 'Keep calm and carry on' may be a nice sentiment, but it is not always an option. So just expect life to hurt us at times – much like a dodgem at a fairground.

Stop Me if You Think You Have Heard This One Before   31

Try as hard as you can, but you can't get into a dodgem car and not expect to be bumped, but here's what I have learnt: the more you are hit the wiser you become. You quickly learn how to manoeuvre yourself out of the way to avoid full impact next time. It's called survival!

Interruptions happen and it is never a case of 'if' but 'when', but we can take some steps to help how we prepare to lessen future shocks that come with knocks.

Several years ago, I went on a Christmas work outing to a go-karting track. But before we were all let loose, we had to hear a safety talk. Then we had to be kitted out with specially padded clothing and helmets before being led to our go karts. It felt a little over the top, but when another colleague came late, missed the safety talk, got kitted up wrongly and ended up with three cracked ribs spoiling his Christmas, we got it!

I am pretty sure he wouldn't do that again and neither would any of us be even tempted to cut corners in the future. This is how we learn and grow. We try to anticipate something trying to hurt us again, by growing in wisdom and learning from past mistakes. But remember too that the thing that bumps you off course could just be your opportunity to change.

We may not have control over the outside forces of interruption, but it is within all of us to take better control of how we act.

When we recognise that some things in life cannot be totally dodged, we get a glimpse into how God is at work in our circumstances. Look closely and you might even see him with you in your 'dodgem car'.

Those times when we experience continual knocks and bumps are maybe when God is wanting to speak to us, to give us directions, in order for something to change.

GO SLOW TO GO FURTHER

To progress we will need to allow for greater spaces for all types of interruptions in our life. The Holy Spirit will use these times to see how any wilfulness in us to do things our own way, pushing us away from God, can be replaced with willingness, which happens when we enter those intimate times with God.

It helps us become aware that there is something better than our ego, something that will bring a greater freedom than any of our best efforts. The noise around us becomes silenced by his stillness and we begin to understand in our hearts the profound and deeply satisfying joy of a surrendered life in Jesus.

Maybe this stillness will present itself with a new song of salvation, or healing, or even a song of lamentation, but your first decision is to agree that you need stopping more than you think, and finding a way to interrupt yourself before something else does it for you.

I say this to help you grasp that God has made you a limited edition of one. There is only one of you.[6] We are all wonderfully and fearfully made in the image of God, unique with immense value. No two people share the same fingerprints.

You are a one-off, a treasured creation, so treat yourself with huge respect, because while your time on earth is limited the blessings of God are not.

MAKING THE DASH COUNT

There are usually two dates on a gravestone. Both have a role to play in giving a life a beginning and an end, but the poet Linda Ellis says in her poem it is the single dash in between that is most important. It represents our values, successes, achievements, failures, relationships, anniversaries, family, ambitions and dreams. Ellis poignantly writes: 'For it matters not how much we own, the cars . . . the house . . . the cash. What matters most is how we live and love and spend our dash.'[7]

But it can feel that this small unassuming dash is a poor return for all the hard work and effort we have put into life. Mark Batterson puts our mortality in an even more sober light than that: 'I'm not convinced that your date of death is the date carved on your tombstone. Most people die long before that. We start dying when we have nothing worth living for. And we don't really start living until we find something worth dying for.'[8] And isn't that the point?

Unless we find time to pause and stop along the way and have a revelation of what life is about, time will continue to be stolen from underneath our feet. As Jesus says, 'The thief comes only to steal and kill and destroy' which makes me appreciate even more that he says in the same breath, 'I have come that they may have life, and have it to the full.'[9]

Stop Me if You Think You Have Heard This One Before   33

Mark was one of my best friends. He died after a courageous battle with cancer. We were of a similar age. He left us far too early, but he typified to me a life lived to the full. His love for Jesus, his wife Sue, children, grandchildren and friends are all testament to that.

It was never the size of his business, bank account or house that impressed me. It was how he lived out his life in the various stages of illness. I seldom saw self-pity or bitterness, although I am sure he must have had some very dark days.

In each selfie he took in hospital Mark almost always seemed to manage a smile, at least a little. However, I feel sure that if he was to measure his life's achievements without faith, grace or gratitude he would have undoubtedly taken quite different pictures of himself.

Cancer disrupted everything: his family life, work life and spiritual life. Yet with each round of treatment, I saw his faith grow stronger, not weaker. His courage and tenacity shone through. Mark made his dash not just a marker of time spent on earth, but of a life lived well, albeit shorter than we all would have wanted.

The disruption was of course not in Mark's game plan, but I have seen how other people have lived much longer and had less gratitude for what they have got.

Some of us will have studied hard, maybe even been fortunate to have gone to university. We have taken on a student loan debt, worked long hours, made huge sacrifices. We might have raised a family, managed to pay off the mortgage, paid into a private pension – and all in the name of comfort and security.

So let me ask you the question: What do you want your dash on your tombstone to say about you when the time comes?

LIVING A LIFE TO BE FORGOTTEN

I grew up in a small village on the outskirts of west London where my bedroom overlooked a graveyard. My father often joked, and I mean often, that it was the dead centre of the village. (It took me a while to get the joke!) One afternoon I took a walk around the gravestones. There are some famous people buried in there, such as members of the local aristocracy as well as the odd metaphysical poet and politician.

34 *Life, Interrupted*

Their names are all carved in either fine marble or granite, some with accompanying angels guarding their tombs, but tucked away at the far end of the graveyard, out of sight, is a cluster of small, unmarked, wooden crosses. You can easily miss them due to the overgrown trees and shrubs. This was where the nuns of the local convent were buried.

You will find no names. And if that was not humbling enough, each cross had buried beneath it not the remains of one nun, but three; each one placed on top of the other. Even in death there was an expectation in the community you continue to share with someone else.

Brother Andrew, founder of Open Doors, in his later years said, 'I live my life to be forgotten.'[10] No memorial to his life achievements was expected. These anonymous nuns have certainly done that. But most of us will probably want our lives to be worth something when our times comes.

As a 12-year-old boy inspecting the graveyard, I somehow managed to grasp that life is sacred. There is nothing wrong about being remembered by name, but there could be a question mark over what we should be remembered for!

My father told me he always enjoyed funerals, which might sound an odd thing to say, but it was because it was often only on these occasions that he got to see all sides of the person and what they had done. Also, to catch up with other long-lost friends.

WHAT CONSTITUTES A LIFE ACHIEVEMENT?

The unknown nuns with their simple wooden markers are a continual interrupter to my thoughts as I grow older. I have wondered how many times they may have got down on their knees to pray. They would have prayed the offices several times in a day over many years. Non-stop.

For a person of no faith, that may seem like a complete waste of a life. After all, these women have forsaken the opportunities of a career, owning a home, marrying and having children.

In my teens I met some of the nuns from the convent. I did not see bitterness or regret in their faces. Quite the opposite. I saw contentment and at times sheer joy. And the peace . . . well, it was something else.

Stop Me if You Think You Have Heard This One Before   35

That is not to say they never argued or fell out with each other, but they all had something in common, they all allowed for the interruptive nature of the Holy Spirit to lead them into a life of contentment through prayer and service to Jesus.

Even though at the time I had no meaningful relationship with God, I understood something of the value of a celebrated life through these wonderful, sacrificial, faith-filled women. If they would allow themselves to be remembered for anything I hope it would be how they continually surrendered their worldly thoughts and ambitions to find an expressive and satisfying relationship with Jesus. No small thing.

However, without the promise of reward of an eternity in the company of Jesus, the wooden cross would seem a poor return for a lifetime of sacrifice and pain. In fact, plain foolishness.

HOW TO PRESS ON WELL

We will all have our avoidance strategies where we try and do anything to eliminate an impending threat to us. If you have children, maybe you have noticed their tactics for avoiding tidying up their bedroom or helping with house chores. There can be such creativity in our children! It seems to be based on their own terms, in their own time, but never ours.

There is an in-built deep need always to want to be in control of what's coming up, but there are many times when life does not play by 'Queensbury rules' and we are left wrong-footed and reeling with the consequences. What is more, we are left in confusion about which direction to go in and which action we should take.

We had moved to Sudbury in East Anglia to plant a church. It is a market town on the Suffolk/Essex border, famous for the River Stour, Sir Thomas Gainsborough, silk mills and its surrounding water meadows.

Having just 'upped sticks' from Twickenham in west London with its cultivated royal parks, I decided I needed to establish a new jogging route. I thought, what could be more scenic than running across the historic water meadows? I set off and began jumping over the odd, small, muddy puddle but, as my run progressed, so did the size and number of puddles. At first it just took more physical energy to avoid the water or to jump across. After all, I like a challenge.

36   *Life, Interrupted*

But ten minutes in, with more wheezing than usual, I had to concede defeat. I also felt the need to apologise to the early morning dog-walkers who had to endure far from graceful acrobatic jumping with unusual grunts and groans.

Of course, I had not understood one important thing: Sudbury's water meadows are named 'water meadows' for a reason. The ground gets very wet, very quickly, with its high water table. It doesn't take much to flood the ancient common land. Any experienced local would have known this. I would have known it too if I had stopped and thought about it more before setting off.

Pressing on regardless is not always the best advice. Of course, it feels as though it should be. It sounds noble and not just a little bit heroic, but there are many times when it can be best described as just plain stupid. I, myself, make the point. You are welcome.

Consider for a moment Paul the apostle's sporting metaphor: 'I press on towards the goal to win the prize for which God has called me heavenwards.'[11] We can be tempted, even conditioned, to read his words as:

Don't lose all the gains you have made.

Don't slip back and regret it.

Set your face like flint.

Citizenship awaits you in heaven.

Keep doing your daily quiet times.

Keep reading your Bible top to bottom, left to right.

Keep serving.

Keep giving.

Keep praying.

Keep going to church.

Keep your chin up.

Keep being Mother Teresa, Billy Graham or your other favourite Christian pin-up.

Our winning strategy is one of 'keeping on keeping on' because, well, it was the advice we inherited. The problem is our efforts never quite satisfy the soul because they are led by a need to perform and always produce results.

Stop Me if You Think You Have Heard This One Before   37

We can read Paul's concept of maturity in his letter to the Philippians as meaning all our hard work and effort is what will see us through come the day when we stand before the mercy seat. Somehow, we think we need to continue to live up to that standard as an encouragement to others. And so, the whole thing perpetuates.

That sounds exhausting. Don't we want to find a better way to live that still has all the benefits of dying to self and living a life in Christ? Besides, is that what Paul is really saying?

Without knowing the context of his life struggles it would be very easy to paint the apostle as a first-century superhero of the faith.

Paul writes his letter as someone not in trainers but in chains. He resides in a Roman prison, not in the comfort of his own home. He is awaiting trial. He does not expect a good outcome. Life is subject to constraints, quite literally. He simply does not have a say in what happens next and yet somehow his letters are still filled with a sense of freedom, contentment and joy.

Even though he was a Pharisee of the law, turned follower of the Way, Paul discovered that identity and self-worth were not shaped by work without distraction, but by finding joy amid the disruptions. He was someone who learnt to live within the limits of the constant stops and starts alongside a carefully planned missionary itinerary. That deserves a cheer!

If you are someone already feeling distracted and that your life is being forced another way, this is what I have picked up from Paul's writings, and it's important to hear even if you never get to another chapter:

You only become

resilient in faith

when your life

is interrupted,

again and

again and

again and

again . . .

Interruptions are your invitation to learn resilience with the purpose of becoming a content and joyful person in Christ.

Character is forged through your present predicament and never in 'peace time', because you and I know that faith untested leads to no faith at all. Each one of life's twists and turns will help see confidence rise, along with courage to be able to handle the next curveball. Resilience will begin to grow within, even when it is not always visible to others.

ROOTS AND SHOOTS

A friend of mine was visiting a vineyard with her husband and asked the owner how the vines were able to survive the long, hot, dry, summer weather. The owner told her it was not a problem because their roots can go down five metres to find water helping provide the necessary nutrients to keep it healthy and alive.

On the surface, the vine may look fragile and unable to cope with the extremities of the weather. Sometimes the fruit will suffer, but more often than not the vine will survive and will produce fruit for the next season.

There will always be setbacks, those times when it feels as though life has become too much for us, but a faith with deep roots will ensure we can recover. And the best way to ensure our roots keep going down to find the water of life is to keep cultivating a heart of gratitude towards Jesus in every trying situation, just as Paul encourages the Christians to do at Colossae: 'So then, just as you received Christ Jesus as Lord, continue to live your lives in him, rooted and built up in him, strengthened in the faith as you were taught, and overflowing with thankfulness.'[12]

Every prayer of gratitude in every circumstance is a step forward against the same disruption ever having the same impact on you again.

But you will need to stop, interrupt yourself, and form new daily habits. As John Maxwell says, 'You will never change your life until you change something you do daily.'[13] That means learning new disciplines to be able to renew the mind to begin to free yourself from those unhelpful thought patterns that want to distract you from finding peace in a Christ-centred relationship. But something will need to be surrendered first.

So much of today's western advice is set around mindfulness and a form of Buddhism which encourages us to empty our minds to find inner peace, but that couldn't be further from the Christian message.

When Paul the apostle talks about how Jesus emptied himself on the cross, it is for the purpose of our salvation. He emptied himself of all divine privileges, such as status and reputation, to enable him to be used by the Father so we can be filled with his glory. Just read that again. That is phenomenal, but it will require us to empty ourselves – and not to stay empty. Our hands need to let go whatever is in them for something better to be put in their place, something of immeasurably more value – the promised gift of forgiveness, new life and an eternal hope.

INTERRUPTER

A DAILY PRAYER TO BREAK UNHEALTHY HABITS

Lord Jesus, give me eyes to see just one change today.

Interrupt my thoughts to unlearn unhealthy ways.

Help me to be courageous in my choices and to see you at work in me.

Holy Spirit, as I raise my dirty hands before you now, cleanse me and fill me with your love, and bring a lasting hope and joy to my soul.

Amen.

4 GIVE YOURSELF A BREAK

I have never been big into tiny insects. Nothing personal you understand but, you know, they are small and to my mind don't really have much entertainment value. Some creep and crawl. Others bite and sting, but the very little ones? I don't want to sound harsh, but are really not worth much attention.

Or so I thought.

When the children were young, we took them to a zoo. Like many zoos, it included a reptile house, which was also home to some pretty strange bugs and amphibians. If honest, I found it an unpleasant, humid, dark building so, on a hot summer day, I was not planning to be in there for too long.

But as I strolled past one particular glass case, with its flickering blue neon light that intermittently hummed, I noticed how small leaves were moving along a branch all by themselves. It freaked me out!

I drew nearer to the glass and saw the leaves were being carried by ants.

The sign beneath read, 'Leaf-cutter Ants. Origin: South and Central America, Mexico.'

Right in front of me were nature's oldest farmers. And one of the world's oddest miniature societies.

I came to discover that these hugely skilled little members of nature's ecosystem are nothing but extraordinary. Leaf-cutter ants punch way above their weight. In fact, fifty times over. They are exceptionally strong and have the most amazing micro-muscles

"

TO PRAY IS TO WORK, TO WORK IS TO PRAY."
BENEDICTINE MOTTO

"

JESUS CAME AND STOOD AMONG THEM AND SAID, 'PEACE BE WITH YOU!'"
JOHN 20:19

that would leave any Marvel Avenger looking ordinary, bar possibly Ant-Man.

Their teeth resemble a lumberjack's saw and can cut through leaves, flowers and foliage with incredible ease. That is because their jaws have special chainsaw mandibles, which are unique to this species of ant and can vibrate a thousand times per second.[1]

No sooner have they chopped down leaves than they are carrying them back all the way to the colony to fertilise their crops. They put them into piles, much like a compost area in your garden, and leave them there to decompose. In time the leaves will break down and be moved on to the colony's fungus garden.

Leaf-cutter ants will dedicate their whole lives to making sure this fungus garden stays healthy. They will tend this garden by removing fungus weeds much as a human gardener does. Hence the moniker of nature's oldest gardeners.

Ant colonies can house up to ten million ants and because of these large unfathomable numbers it is easy to think each one is essentially the same. But no. Each ant has an important job designated to it, such as a worker, soldier or gardener. One of the most fascinating ones has got to be given to the minim ant.

These are the tiny protectors whose job it is to 'ride shotgun' on the leaves and remove any dangerous parasites *en route* back to the colony. They protect the leaves from flies and wasps, proving the point that size really isn't everything.

These members of this ancient ant society will do this day in, day out, seven days a week, fifty-two weeks of the year. No let-up, which means no time off for Christmas, not even for the kids' nativity play.

Nothing distracts them from doing their job. And if they are interrupted, they will find a way to just carry on. They are the ultimate unstoppable workforce, and probably every boss's dream!

This might sound obvious, but we are not leaf-cutter ants; we are amazing, awe-inspiring, individually made, God-breathed human beings made in the Creator's likeness. We are the apple of his eye, his favoured ones who have been given the privilege of having overall responsibility for his creation, including leaf-cutter ants.

We are not created to be non-stop workers where we have to earn our place in the world. Unlike the ant, we cannot go nineteen to the dozen every second of the day without causing ourselves some serious harm. In fact, unless there are interruptions, such activity will physically kill us.

PRODUCTIVITY VERSUS SATISFACTION

A company director once told me he liked to see all his employees in the office working at their desks. It reassured him they were being productive, and worried him when he couldn't see their progress. I observed over time though how interruptions to this work culture upset him. I noticed how it drove an obsessive behaviour to making strange and, at times, unreasonable decisions. Speaking as a consultant, I gently remarked that perhaps sitting at a desk all day without interruption is not as productive as he might think. I mean anyone can put on a show when the boss is in the room! I suggested that he should judge his employees by their output, not their input. Glad to say things began to change for everyone concerned.

We can easily get paranoid when we can't see what we want to see. Sometimes it is best to make light of it. I suspect it is an apocryphal story, but one CEO is said to have sent around an all-staff email saying, 'Please don't spend all morning looking out of the window, give yourself something to do in the afternoon. Love, your boss.'

Being made to feel you have to be productive doesn't build confidence and trust; it only builds resentment, but still, we think somehow it is our golden ticket to happiness. Maybe at social gatherings we shouldn't just ask someone, 'What do you do?' but also, 'Why do you do it?' And then watch their face.

The thing that will stop us going down a rabbit-hole of busyness without progress is to know our 'why?' before the 'how?' and 'what?'. Our life has got a purpose; it is for us to discover it and then dwell in that place with gratitude to God. It is the one thing that will satisfy the soul and fulfil us. Spend time getting this right and it will start to populate all your thoughts and guide your future actions.

But here's the thing: if we can't learn to stop ourselves, to pause and ask, 'What is my purpose? Why am I here? What is the Lord's best for me?' our next stop could lead to our full stop – our final breath.

We know this to be true. It is why over the years we will have heard it said when speaking about mortality and purpose, 'Nobody on

44   *Life, Interrupted*

their deathbed ever said, "I wish I could have spent more time in the office."'

Archbishop Justin Welby said, 'When we are at the funeral of a loved friend or relative, we hear death saying to us, "I am the final answer. All ends in this complete nothingness and emptiness. Do not deceive yourselves."'[2]

Yet the deception starts while life is in full flow. There is the desire in us that wants to be vindicated for our attitude towards work. But if that is all our life purpose amounts to then something is missing – and death really will have won.

It is as the archbishop says, 'What we see we value. We value wealth that is visible, and life that is confident.'[3] It is why we often see those employees who go the extra mile getting the promotion. Shockingly, one boss told me that he was probably going to have to let one employee go because they wanted to leave work at 5.30 p.m. so they could get home and help their wife bath their baby. I said, 'Is that not a reasonable request?' It was met with derision and laughter.

There is a strong temptation to value the visibility of labour more than an invisible God at work in us – even though one may take your life and the other gives it back.

So we keep going as if everything depends upon us and not if everything depended on God. We keep busy, keep achieving, keep having more, doing all we can to justify our life choices and the way we are. And it will stay this way unless something comes along and knocks it off its perch.

In my first job out of college I worked for a company where there was an unwritten rule that everyone got in at 8.30 a.m. and stayed until at least 7 p.m., which was when the boss left. It was not unusual to stay until 10 p.m. But there is a problem with a working week that doesn't give space to see outside of itself. The soul was never meant to be left alone for six days where God's Spirit is allowed to be pushed to the sides, disregarded and forgotten. When we work under constant pressure with no interruptions, and our days are held together more with angst than the non-anxious presence of Jesus, we lose sight of the centre of our purpose and core being.

Are you starting to see the problem? Our work becomes our worship and pleasure is our reward. Meanwhile, our soul is waiting for us to join him in song.

I know how adept I am at telling myself that 'God understands!' But while we prefer the visible outworking over the invisible grace, because it can feel more productive and tangible, it will leave us eventually being only dissatisfied with our lot. It might offer us dopamine hits but there will be the feeling too that we want the experience to be more consistent and constant and not to fade away at the end of each working day.

Meanwhile our focus on success is like living in a trench; we are failing to see what else is around us. It is what makes King Solomon's wisely spoken words nearly three thousand years ago so shatteringly pertinent for our phone-scrolling, fast-moving, Instagram-living generation: 'Where there is no vision, the people perish.'[4]

I take that vision to mean that when we see God and see ourselves as God sees us – which includes how we see our work, relationships, money and possessions – only then will we get clarity to live our visible life well. But unless we find a way to interrupt ourselves, we will remain blind, unseeing of just how rich our life can really be, leaving us with less than a full picture of what it is to be made in the image of God.

How we move forward will depend on how much we allow our busy space to be interrupted and to still have hearts that listen. As the German mystic Meister Ekhardt observes, 'He who would be serene and pure needs but one thing: detachment.'[5] So here's one very practical way we can begin to do that . . .

- Stop.
- Become still.
- Listen.

FORCED INTERRUPTIONS

If you have just tried that, congratulations. You have just made an important space available in your heart to hear God speak into your life. It might also be the most productive thing you have done today. Because here's the thing: it is the self-enforced stopping that will help us begin to see a vision for our visible and invisible life.

Interruptions are a necessity if we want to see ourselves progress. In racing, F1 drivers are forced to make at least one pit stop to change tyres and refuel before they can go on – such are the needs of the high-performance turbo-charged cars they drive. But it will also need a team to help them get back on track (no pun intended, seriously).

It will need a team around us too. More to the point, we were never meant to do life alone anyway, we were created for relationship, which might come as a relief if you are feeling currently crushed or under-supported and working at turbo-speeds.

It is why sabbaticals, spiritual retreats and pilgrimages, have become so increasingly important in our high-performance lives.

And they are not just for Christians. There are retreats designed for businesses to help employees with increased stress and anxiety levels. According to the Health and Safety statistics, stress, depression or anxiety account for 50 per cent of all work-related ill health cases in 2020/21 and, according to Deloitte, poor mental health costs UK employers up to £56 billion each year. And if you are too busy to come to them, one company will even bring a mobile retreat cabin to you.[6]

RETREATING TO ADVANCE

Signing up to a four-year senior pastors' residential group retreat was one of the best decisions I ever made. No one there could really afford the time, but we all concluded neither could we afford not to be there, there was too much at stake. The enemy always wants to strike the shepherd and scatter the sheep, and an unattended life that neglects the body, mind and spirit will help it along. We all knew that what was good for the pastor was also good for our churches.

One thing is for sure: it shouldn't take a crisis such as a marriage breakdown, serious illness, redundancy or company receivership to make us stop and notice the true state of things, but of course, often it does.

On one retreat away I wrote in my journal a raw confession after I had realised that my busyness to get on was a form of spiritual blindness. Here is an extract:

My rush to get urgent things done has become an obstacle to experiencing the one thing I should desire most, the close company of you, Jesus.

I have not wanted to stop this week. Partly because in the silence I fear what I will find. Being left to my own thoughts feels a dangerous place

Give Yourself a Break

to be. It feels risky and deeply uncomfortable. It makes everything feel real. Intentional. Obvious. It is terrifying. The feeling of empty space has surprised me. It is unexpected grace.

I notice nature through my window.

I notice an empty chair in an empty room with an empty cup.

I notice a mirror.

I notice someone looking back at me, wearing half a disguise.

I notice my mood.

I notice a numbness, an indifference.

I notice my loneliness

I notice I fear being caught doing nothing, even on a retreat.

I notice perhaps too much.

But then I notice you and you see me.

And then I notice what I have always known,

You only see me and you only want me to only see you.

As your psalmist wrote:

'You have searched me, LORD,

and you know me.

You know when I sit and when I rise;

you perceive my thoughts from afar.

Where can I go from your Spirit?

Where can I flee from your presence?'

Psalm 139:1–3,7

Stopping and noticing is as much a spiritual discipline as prayer, fasting and reading the Bible.

This all means we will need to break some patterns of long-held behaviour, as well as maybe our addiction to success.

As much as we want to leave an empty mailbox and answer every email before we finish the day, we can't.

So, stop.

48   *Life, Interrupted*

There will never be enough hours in the day, even if we get new technology in place because we will only learn how to fill our time with something else.

So, stop.

As much as we want something to be perfect and be at its best, putting a lot of extra hours in will move the dial only slightly.

So, stop.

We are never going to earn enough money to buy what we want because there will always be something else that comes along after it.

So, stop.

LISTEN!

One day I was sitting down with Bishop Sandy Millar and telling him how crazy things had got with the church's foodbank and some of my challenges. None of this seemed to be of much interest to him. Instead, he suggested we go for a walk down to the beach. I was still jabbering on about stuff when he stopped and said, 'Can you hear those birds singing? They are all praising God.'

I have got to be honest; it felt a bit trivial compared to what was going on with me, but as we stood and paused I began to listen more intently – and it was truly a beautiful sound. I found it comforting, even restorative. It felt in that moment that my striving for answers was being replaced with worship. And it was welcome.

If we can find the courage to interrupt ourselves and stop – even when it is most inconvenient and feels time is against us – to listen to the voice of God, whether it's through a scene of nature, a Spotify worship playlist, a Bible app or maybe just in the silence and solitude of a quiet space, we will have taken an important step forward in understanding time was never ours to control; it is a gift from our Creator God, a space we get to occupy to bring glory to himself where we are invited to enjoy with him.

The self-enforced interruption will always offer to re-centre our relationship with Jesus to give us an eternal perspective where everything else finds its place around it. It is our worship, our Sabbath, our place of renewal and hope. It is where we hear the birds worshipping and the angels singing. It is the holy ground we walk upon where we experience the eternal flickering presence of God, the One who whispers in the wind and shouts from the cross, 'It is finished.'

Our time becomes his time and, in his presence, it takes on the appearance of eternity in disguise.

INTERRUPTIONS COME WITH MORE GRACE THAN YOU KNOW

Jesus is on a rescue mission and eagerly wants to occupy the space a forced stop creates in us. But if we can stop first and interrupt ourselves it becomes that much easier to be re-centred on his non-anxious presence. He lovingly waits in this space, ready to attend to our needs to remind us of our one true purpose – to be loved and to love.

He longs to lift the veil of our non-stop restlessness and achievement-driven self, our ego, in order to deal with our fear of failure and never being enough and always wanting more. But we are never despised for our poor choices, only pitied and shown compassion over those things that retain a tight grip on our life values. It will demand a sacrifice, but it will be no greater than the sacrifice made for our freedom.

His invisible grace interrupts our visible lives. As Isaiah prophesied, Jesus is sent 'to bind up the broken-hearted, to proclaim freedom for the captives and release the darkness for the prisoners.'[7] That means you and me. The kingdom of God is an endgame in our time, not a future time.

We often hear life described as a merry-go-round, meaning it never stops, not even for a second. It is something we just have to endure and get on with, keeping our heads down to get through it. And it only stops when our time on earth stops. Now that is a pretty grim picture if we had no God of the interruption.

'STOP THE WORLD, I WANT TO GET OFF!'

As a young boy I used to love it when the fair came to my village every spring bank-holiday weekend. It meant I got to ride the vintage merry-go round with its colourfully decorated horses and bright lights. On one occasion a girl younger than me was put on the horse next

50   *Life, Interrupted*

to me. Her face was beaming with joy as she waved to her father on
the side. But as the merry-go-round started to go round faster and
faster, the girl quickly became distressed and began to scream and
cry. I watched her crumble before me, unable to do anything for her.

Then suddenly everything stopped.

The lights went out and the merry-go-round came to a grinding halt.
The small child took her chance and quickly shimmied off the back
of the horse and ran into the arms of her waiting father. If I was
suspicious, I might think the father had gone behind the back of the
operator's booth and pulled out the plug.

Maybe we can identify with that small child and feel like screaming
with the unrelenting pace of life. Maybe we have said in jest, 'Stop the
world, I want to get off!' The good news is that there is always a loving
father waiting nearby with a plan to pull out the plug if we are unable
to stop, and need his assistance.

When finally entering the promised land, Joshua and the people
were reassured God was truly with them. After forty years of relearn-
ing what it is to be free from forced work under a dictator in Egypt,
God used the interruption of the desert to help them visualise their
future with him. He had spoken on every stop of the journey, a journey I am told that takes, on average, only eleven days to walk, so a
lot of stops! It was not time wasted, but time saved. It was the sacred
space to learn faith and to give them confidence to know the Lord
their God was with them wherever they went.[8]

We must accept, though, that the Lord will often choose to do more
behind our back than he shows to our face, but we can be assured
we will always have his full attention, his gaze is always on us. Jesus
says, 'The very hairs of your head are all numbered. Don't be afraid;
you are worth more than many sparrows.'[9]

He knows you better than you do yourself. He knows your deepest
anxieties and what brings you the greatest joy. The non-stop side of
you can stop and be parked up for a new way to begin. That is grace
or, as Paul the apostle reminds us: 'There is now no condemnation
for those who are in Christ.'[10]

I find it reassuring, if sometimes inconvenient, that God sees straight
through my poor thinking, my shoddy excuses and untenable approach to busyness. In the space I make and the time I sacrifice
I see a faithful, loving and kind God with a better vision for my life

than I have, which makes me happy to follow. As Dietrich Bonhoeffer wrote from his prison cell in Nazi Germany: 'God does not give us everything we want, but he does fulfil all his promises, i.e., he remains the Lord of the earth, he preserves his church, constantly renewing our faith and not laying on us more than we can bear, gladdening us with his nearness and help, hearing our prayers and leading us along the best and straightest paths to Himself.'[11]

This is the invisible life made visible. This is true progress being made. When life seems unstoppable, and it will, stop before something else stops you. Give yourself a break.

INTERRUPTER

A PRAYER FOR THE 'TROUBLED WORKER' IN US

Lord Jesus, for my work, rest and play

I ask for your love, joy, and peace.

Your love where I have become anxious or weary with the day.

Your joy when I close my eyes at night.

Your peace when I wake in the morning.

May I trust in your provision and always see you in my workplace and internal space

For me to enjoy the good, the true and the beautiful through the one who makes all things new.

Amen.

5 USE YOUR IMAGINATION!

I had just landed a job working for a large advertising agency in Covent Garden, London. It even came with its own office, of sorts, albeit opposite the men's toilets on the third floor. But it mattered not as on a warm summer's day I could open my window and hear the English National Opera rehearse next door above the flushing of loos and hand-dryer noise. I was living the dream!

I can't say that everyone thought my career choice was a good one as at the time the company Saatchi & Saatchi shone a somewhat negative light on the industry with its 'yuppy' image of affluence. It made me aware of Jacques Seguela's book title: *Don't Tell My Mother I'm in Advertising – She Thinks I Play the Piano in a Brothel*.

I was also quite a young Christian and still trying to figure out how to live for Jesus and exist in the world of advertising while surrounded by creative egos and Italian knitwear.

A friend and I decided in late August to take a week's holiday in the Highlands of Scotland. Along the way we booked ourselves in for a couple of nights at a guest-house in a small village near to the steep-sided Glencoe valley – a truly beautiful area known for its waterfalls and climbing peaks, and congeniality around the pool table in the local pub.

The tourist walks leaflet didn't disappoint. We chose a path and climbed to the top with views that were simply breathtaking.

> **THERE ARE COSTS AND RISKS TO A PROGRAM OF ACTION, BUT THEY ARE FAR LESS THAN THE LONG-RANGE RISKS AND COSTS OF COMFORTABLE INACTION."**
> JOHN F. KENNEDY[1]

> **I DO BELIEVE; HELP ME OVERCOME MY UNBELIEF!"**
> AN ANXIOUS FATHER IN NEED OF A MIRACLE[2]

It was in this moment that I declared to my friend how great God is. A minute of silence followed before he said, 'Andrew, if God took away your job, would you still worship him?'

'Of course!' I chirped.

Undented, if caught a little off guard and feeling offended by the question, I stood on that mountain feeling triumphant and self-satisfied. If I had been wearing a red cloak with a big 'S' on a blue T-shirt it wouldn't have looked out of place.

But three months later that mountain-top conversation would come back to haunt me. A massive interruption was waiting to break into the plans I had prepared for my life. Not only would it affect my future career path, but also everything else that I had put my trust and confidence in.

It was a Monday morning in late October when I was summoned to see the CEO. I was ushered into his spacious corner suite where I was shown to a low reclining sofa. Its chic Milano design meant my knees were almost as high as my chest, but I did my best to look casual and attentive. This was the holiest of holy offices, which made it all the more an intimidating experience for someone like me.

I was then informed of the current difficulties caused by the recession, market forces and how clients were cutting budgets. Thus the company was forced to make some tough and unpleasant decisions. One of those meant letting me go.

As I sat in stunned silence trying to take in the worst news possible, I heard the steady chink of coins beginning to fall out of one of my trouser pockets only to see them sliding down the back of the black leather sofa. For some inexplicable reason, at that precise moment, it felt more important to rescue the loose change than to challenge the decision to let me go.

I was no doubt in a state of shock, but looking back I do wonder if in some strange way rescuing my loose change wasn't a metaphor for trying to hold onto some man-made security.

When life goes well it is easy to worship God. It is also incredibly easy to say encouraging things to others from this vantage point, a place of plenty. You have noticed that too, I am sure.

We feel super-strong and super-confident.

Use Your Imagination! 55

We may even feel ourselves becoming a sort of superhero in the faith and begin to see how it is a duty, a calling, to be this version of ourselves to help pull others through but, as I discovered, it doesn't take much of an interruption to bring this perspective on life crashing down.

SUPER-SPECIAL OR SUPER-ORDINARY

In the last few decades, we have seen comic book superheroes brought to the big, and small, screen and I must admit I have seen most films and TV episodes at least once. In fact, *Agents of S.H.I.E.L.D.* helped keep me going through the Covid-19 pandemic.

One of the reasons why I believe this genre is so popular is because we all wish we could be like them, someone different, someone not like us. We like the idea that one minute our superheroes are normal regular people like us and the next they are saving the world.

Comic book heroes fall into the category of fantasy, but for a while it used to be seen as a subset of science fiction, but both are about imagining the improbable. Fantasy is defined as having thoughts from the conscious or subconscious with no basis in reality. But I wonder if it can be an aid to helping us live with reality while waiting to see a better future. Hang in there, let me explain.

There are times when fantasy is used to survive a situation. I remember being incredibly moved by Roberto Benigni's film, *Life is Beautiful*, which is about an Italian Jewish bookstore owner who uses his child's innocent imagination to protect him from seeing the horrors of the Nazi occupation. Considering the grimness of the subject matter, it manages to be both funny and sad – right up until the end. Quite a feat!

Of course, our experience with fantasy is not always positive. We all know when we have met a fantasist, not least when a 'Walter Mitty' type person comes up to you at church and says God has told them to build an ark in their back garden or wants you to follow them after the service to a graveyard to raise the recently deceased.

There is perhaps something in all of us that wants to be awed, astonished and amazed by something greater than ourselves. We are open to the impossible because many of us face impossible situations. We yearn for something special to interrupt the harsh reality of our daily difficulties.

56   *Life, Interrupted*

Psychologists say fantasy is critical in the development and exercising of a child's imagination. Fantasy does nothing less than feed our sense of wonder. It gives our minds permission to explore at a safe distance the big concepts such as life, death, war, greed, suffering, pain, etc. – all which have the power to affect our emotional wellbeing.

C.S. Lewis and his fellow Inkling, J.R.R. Tolkien, both used the genre of fantasy, inspired by Greek and Nordic myths, to explore important themes in their other worlds of Narnia and Middle Earth. In Tolkien's trilogy, apart from a cracking good story, he explores the human struggles of good and evil, life and death, fate and free will, but his biggest theme is death and immortality.

It is hard not see the Lord of the Rings series as a parable or commentator on modern life, not least when you hear of tech billionaires, the super-rich, wanting to use their wealth to help humans 'cheat death'. Clearly, they disagree with the poet Alfred Lord Tennyson's view that 'all things must die'.[3]

The writer of Ecclesiastes wrote with beautiful human insight thousands of years before: 'There is a time for everything, and a season for every activity under the heavens: a time to be born and a time to die.'[4]

Death is involuntary as much as our birth is involuntary, but much of what happens in between is up for grabs.

Powerful stories of the imagination like those set in Middle Earth or in the Narnian chronicles give us time and space to learn how to respond to real problems. It is a place to pause before the rest of life begins.

However, there is a difference in the world of imagination between fantasy and dreams. They can seem very similar in our minds but have quite different impacts upon us.

DREAMS THAT INTERRUPT OUR AWAKE MOMENTS

Dreams can inspire us to achieve great things, while the fantasies in our heads tend to be egocentric and serve only our own desires, such as sexual fantasies and escapism. As the writer of Proverbs says, 'Those who chase fantasies will have their fill of poverty.'[5]

Use Your Imagination! 57

However, I can't help but think how difficult it must have been for Joseph's eleven brothers to hear how in his dream the sun, moon and eleven stars were all bowing down to him. It must have sounded fantastical and not just a little egotistical.[6]

But, overall, as Christians we are much more comfortable with the language of dreams. Although, if you have come from a traditional conservative evangelical background like mine there can be a wariness around anything that looks mystical, psychic and a little 'off the wall'.

We can be sceptical about those things that don't have a key Bible verse to explain the human experience. And, of course, all experiences of the conscious or unconscious need to be checked against something, which is why when interpreting dreams and visions we like to ask: Does this sound like the character of God and how he likes to do things?

A.W. Tozer knew some exercises of the imagination, such as trying to understand what it means to be made in the image of God, can be dangerous. He thought we run the risk of bringing God down to our own level of understanding for our own manageable needs – such are our human limitations.

> When we try to imagine what God is like we must out of necessity use that which is not God as the raw material for our mind to work on; hence whatever we visualise God to be, He is not, for we have constructed our image out of that which He has made and what He has made is not God. If we insist upon trying to imagine Him, we end with an idol, made not with hands but with thoughts; and an idol of the mind is as offensive to God as an idol of the hand.[7]

But let's not be afraid of the imagination breaking into our reality, let's redeem it.

Throughout the Bible, dreams and visions often pop up whenever God wants to say something important and change the path of current experience and expectation. They help us see that it is more than okay to interrupt the flow of life with the imaginative tools of dreams and visions. What's more, my own experiences have shown that God will use them powerfully to fulfil his purposes and extend his kingdom on earth.

Jacob's dream at Bethel is just one interruption.

58   *Life, Interrupted*

He had a dream in which he saw a stairway resting on the earth, with its top reaching to heaven, and the angels of God were ascending and descending on it. There above it stood the LORD, and he said: 'I am the LORD, the God of your father Abraham and the God of Isaac. I will give you and your descendants the land on which you are lying. Your descendants will be like the dust of the earth, and you will spread out to the west and to the east, to the north and to the south. All peoples on earth will be blessed through you and your offspring. I am with you and will watch over you wherever you go, and I will bring you back to this land. I will not leave you until I have done what I have promised you.'

Genesis 28:12–15

Without faith this could have been seen as fantasy yet, because Jacob believed in God, he took it to heart to be true. The dream was not just about him; it was about a whole people who were yet to be born. It had excitement, adventure, direction and purpose. Up to this point, Jacob had acted less than honourably with his brother and family, but God stands by his promises made to Abraham and begins to speak to Jacob of a future filled with an abundance of blessing.[8]

Emma and I were considering what to do with our lives next. At the time we were part of an amazing church leadership team at a new Anglican church plant in Twickenham, west London. It was a comfortable place to be, not least because I often joked it was near my beloved football club in Stamford Bridge. Unlike Jacob, I was not in a desperate place, financially or relationally, and could easily just keep doing what I was doing. We had bought a family house and our girls loved their school. We had made some good friends. Life was pretty good.

But one Sunday morning as I sat in the front pew, I felt unusually fidgety, before becoming increasingly restless in myself. It began to distract me, which is not good when you are supposed to be leading a service.

I remember saying to Jesus under my breath, 'I want to do more, there must be more, show me what I can do? I am here!'

Around a year later, one Saturday night I got the call!

It became a huge interruption, which would see the next stage of our lives released – and it came in the most unexpected way.

I dreamt that Emma, the girls and I were living in a place called Sudbury. The name was crystal clear. I could even visualise this place. We seemed happy and fulfilled living there.

Use Your Imagination! 59

I got up early the next morning having clearly remembered the details of the dream, so much so that I just needed to get into the study and find the AA Travel map book (for younger readers, these were the days before Google Maps). I looked up 'Sudbury' and saw one near Wembley, but my spirit told me that was not it. Then I saw 'Sudbury, Suffolk'.

As soon as I saw this page a memory was unlocked.

We had once got lost trying to get back to the M11 from our friends' home in Bury St Edmunds. They were known to us from my time on staff at Riverside Vineyard and we had confided in them a while ago that we thought we could be moving but didn't know where. They had suggested planting a church in East Anglia, but at the time I joked and said I could never move there because there was no Caffè Nero. Yes, I was that shallow!

We had got lost going home that weekend and drove unknowingly into the town of Sudbury. Emma never saw it as she had a migraine and was asleep for a lot of the car journey.

But it gets spookier!

On that same Sunday morning Emma strolls into the study and sees that I have the map book out and asks me what I am doing. I tell her, 'Oh, just doing some admin!' I know, lame.

'Last night I had the most extraordinary dream,' she said. 'I dreamt we were living in a place called Sudbury. I saw myself walking down the high street with the girls.'

I was stunned! I came clean and shared my dream and we just looked at each other and laughed.

LONGING FOR AN INTERRUPTION

It was the break our hearts were longing for – even if our minds didn't know the detail. An interruption that would lead to an adventure, but it just didn't come as we might have expected.

The call to plant a church didn't conveniently start with a Scripture being highlighted in my daily devotions, a word from someone at the front or a picture from a home group, it was a dream.

Now, here's the thing, I have never had a dream like it since. I am not even someone who really dreams anyway, come to that. In fact, so

60   *Life, Interrupted*

far, it has been a one-off, but neither of us could deny it was God. In the coming weeks we read the Bible stories of others who had dreams and it began to dawn on me that dreams give birth to seeing new nations emerge and people being saved and restored to the glory of God. Our two dreams started to feel more and more like the kind of thing God might do.

To cut a long but exciting story short, by August 2005, we had moved, lock, stock and barrel, to Sudbury in south Suffolk.

Two years later Stour Valley Vineyard Church was planted in the town with two eager faith-filled new pastors, three young girls, two rabbits and a cheap laptop, courtesy of Vineyard Churches. Today it continues to grow through a shared vision with like-minded people and has seen thousands of lives changed and given hope through our compassion programme – all in the name of Jesus. It really has been a huge privilege and one of the most glorious interruptions to our rather ordinary, normal, everyday lives.

The church in Sudbury is proof that dreams can influence our waking lives, not least when they are supernatural, given by the Holy Spirit. What's more, it should tell us that Jesus is for the church and loves our neighbours as much as he loves us. We remember always the church was one of his oldest and best ideas and pastors just get to hold the keys for a while.

BUILDING A VISION THROUGH DREAMS

Before Emma and I started, we took plenty of time out to try and imagine what kind of church the Lord might want to build. It was fun – and a little bit scary, all at the same time!

A new friend who later became one of our trustees gave me a book called *A Forgotten Revival*. It was the historic account of the East Anglian revival of 1921, which started in Lowestoft and found its way over to Ireland and Scotland through fishermen.

I had thought I was pretty much up on spiritual awakenings in the UK, but this book was a real eye-opener and just another interrupter in my plans on how to build a church. Local church historian, Stanley Griffin, gives an extraordinary account of revival coming to the seaside town on the East coast.

He tells for instance how an awesome awareness of God accompanied the preaching of Jock Troup at Yarmouth during the herring season. God came down into the market place after the stalls had closed and strong fishermen fell to the ground under conviction of sin, while others knelt in the street in the rain. Fisher-girls were similarly affected and unable to work in the curing yards until they were right with God; and men were saved out on the sea, miles from the preaching.

Stanley Griffin concludes, 'It is an important principle of revival that while it is always preceded by prayer, it does not originate with prayer but with God.'[9]

Stories like this can send our imagination into overdrive. We can start thinking, 'If Jesus has done this once, why not again?'

I don't know about you, but I long for our imperfect, best-intentioned plans to be interrupted by more Holy Ghost stories like these. I desire to see more of these divine interventions breaking into ordinary lives, to rescue the lost and broken, to bring hope and healing for many searching people for them to enter into a vibrant and dynamic relationship with Jesus.

Places like Lowestoft, Great Yarmouth or Sudbury don't feel like obvious places to be called to serve, I have since discovered. You will know what I mean if you have ever visited these places but, thank God, the Holy Spirit does not share our perspective or prejudices. I remember vividly a retired vicar saying to us not long after we had moved to the town, 'Why on earth would you want to come to Sudbury? It's a hell-hole!'

They were shattering words from someone who had served the area for many years, but I thought afterwards, 'Well, then, we will just have to love the hell out of Sudbury.'

In the months that followed we began to imagine what our first fifty people would look like. We imagined marriages being restored, long-term addictions broken, and kindness being poured into every crack of our community through social programmes. We wanted it to be a place of everyday miracles, signs and wonders, creating a sacred safe space where all were welcome to come as they were.

We also knew that we were entering a spiritual battle, but we took as our encouragement stories such as the one of Joshua's armies

62   *Life, Interrupted*

marching around the ancient city of Jericho seven times and demolishing its intimidating, high, fortress walls. We had to imagine the impossible was not impossible.

When vision is lacking, it is easy to talk yourself out of having any expectation of a God of wonder, which is why we need a God of signs to make us wonder all the more.

How easy it is to say to ourselves that it is best to be realistic and not to expect too much. We can even find ourselves backtracking with vision when conversations start with 'Historically, this is a spiritually hard area to do church in'.

These comments, however well-intentioned, interrupt vision, bring indecision and put limitations on how we expect to see God move. He has shown us already that he is more than capable of conquering death and rising from the grave, so why wouldn't he raise hope elsewhere? If good can come out of Nazareth and Lowestoft, good can come out of where you live too.

DREAMING THE IMPOSSIBLE

Leo Burnett, the founder of a global advertising agency I once worked at, said, 'Reach for the stars. You might not get one, but neither will you come up with a handful of mud.'[10]

Dreaming the impossible is not being irresponsible, it is about being faithful to the testament of God. It is giving life to an irresistible urge to release faith to see change. No wonder Vineyard Churches in the UK use Dreaming the Impossible as the name of its youth national summer gatherings to inspire faith to help see change for the church and the communities they reside in.

Because 'all things are possible,' right?

At our church we used a version of words borrowed and adapted from our friend Dave Workman who pastored a large church in Cincinnati, Ohio, to describe the kind of community we want to see for ourselves and for our community:

Imagine . . . a motley collection of ordinary people who are on a journey of surrender and transformation through the grace of God.

They choose to be real with him and real with one another.

They are generous and compassionate; no strings attached.

Use Your Imagination! 63

They are grace-givers, hope-bringers, wide-eyed dreamers and risk-takers.

They laugh together, cry together, worship together and serve together.

They know that little things done with great love will change their community, starting with themselves.

They are us.

We have shared these words every time we have held a newcomers' lunch and asked our guests if it sounds like the kind of church they could join. Most of them have said how they have found them inspiring and speak of being in a 'real' community of believers. They are comments that cry out for an authentic faith.

One of my other American pastor friends says, 'People want to know if you smoke what you grow' (a reference to tobacco, not the medicinal plant, I believe!), meaning: Do your words have any value beyond retweeted sayings and Instagram quotes? Are they something you truly believe in deep down in your soul?

But it all starts with the word 'imagine' – an invitation to paint a picture in the mind's eye of what God's vision could mean for our lives.

THE POWER OF IMAGINATION OVER REASON

I am pretty sure that the first rocket to the moon did not start with a dry scientific conversation at Monday morning's staff time. It most likely started with imagination – a fantasy – maybe even inspired from something out of the *Boy's Own* annual, which featured science fiction writers such as Jules Verne and Sir Arthur Conan Doyle.[11]

The two brothers, Wilbur and Orville Wright, were inspired as young children in their playtime to invent the plane – all from their active imaginations. Thank goodness Xbox was not around then!

When their father, Milton, brought home a rubber band-powered toy helicopter, something was sparked in them. As they played with the toy, they saw how it flew across the room before eventually hitting a light fitting and coming crashing to the floor.

The two boys never forgot this playtime moment, it stuck in their minds. However, it would be another sixty years until the toy helicopter itself turned from fantasy to fact with the VS-300 designed by Igor Sikorsky in 1939.

64   *Life, Interrupted*

You are probably aware of the phrase 'flight of fancy', which is used to dismiss a story or idea as being too outlandish to be believed. But by quickly rejecting something because it possibly interferes with our world-view, we might miss out seeing a move of God under our very noses. And no one wants to be the equivalent of Decca Records who passed on signing up the Beatles.

Zechariah, the husband of Elizabeth, is one person who caught the moment. When the angel of the Lord interrupted him while serving in the temple he was understandably filled with fear:

> Do not be afraid, Zechariah; your prayer has been heard. Your wife Elizabeth will bear you a son, and you are to call him John. He will be a joy and delight to you, and many will rejoice because of his birth, for he will be great in the sight of the Lord. He is never to take wine or other fermented drink, and he will be filled with the Holy Spirit even before he is born. He will bring back many of the people of Israel to the Lord their God. And he will go on before the Lord, in the spirit and power of Elijah, to turn the hearts of the parents to their children and the disobedient to the wisdom of the righteous – to make ready a people prepared for the Lord.

Luke 1:13–17

The problem for Zechariah was that he believed in God, his heavenly realm, but had no understanding of how the Creator God, the God of Moses and Elijah, could overrule the physical improbability of his wife having a child in old age. Quite simply, he did not know what to do with an interruption of this magnitude brought by this celestial being. Even though you would have thought an angel turning up would have helped! 'Zechariah asked the angel, "How can I be sure of this? I am an old man and my wife is well along in years."'[12]

It is not that they hadn't tried. You can understand the logic at work here. If they had not been able to conceive when Elizabeth was younger, what chance was there now that she was in her old age? How could God now interrupt the story written over their lives, the one in which they were known among their friends as the couple who couldn't conceive?

One of my ongoing joys is seeing lives transformed through God's mercy and kindness where there is hidden pain and disappointment. We can often put on our 'game face' and go to church and say what we need to say, doing what we need to do while inside our true emotions are suppressed, believing it is better not to share them with others. I suspect many people choose to think, as my sport friends do

Use Your Imagination! 65

when watching the England Cricket Team play Australia, it is better not to hope, because it is the hope that kills you.

But in the kingdom of God that is a lie, and one I find that we are happy to believe at times. Yet are we so filled with low expectations that we can no longer believe that God will break into our secular culture, let alone imagine a future where he is victorious over all battles of the heart and mind?

If we want to imagine the church as the disrupter of the patterns of confusion, shame and pain in our communities, we will probably first need to see old patterns of unbelief disrupted in us. We will need to experience more of God's profound love being poured out through acts of kindness. We will need to see signs and wonders, and miracles. We will need to have the confidence to be different and stand apart. It is what makes our own stories of hope so important.

THE MULTIPLICATION OF A MODERN MIRACLE

Carl and Emma had just started coming to church when one morning I felt the Lord give me a 'word of knowledge'. I remember going across to where they were sitting and saying , 'The Lord says, "You will!"' And that was pretty much it.

I have had to learn to live with the limited words on telegrams from heaven, frustrating as it can be at times when you wish you could say more. However, if it is from God, it is always more than enough.

Sometime later we invited our friend, Sandy Millar, to speak at church. He told the story of how John Wimber, the founder of the Vineyard movement, had spoken one Sunday evening at Holy Trinity, Brompton, and had a word for a woman in the room who was desperate to have a baby but couldn't conceive. He prophesied that she would become pregnant and give birth.

Nine months later the woman gave birth to a beautiful baby boy.

On hearing the story, Carl and Emma got out of their seats at the end of the service and asked Sandy to pray for them. A year later they were proud parents of a baby boy. Prayer really is the gift that keeps on giving, but it was imagination, coupled with faith, that allowed them to believe it could also happen to them. The Lord loves to multiply a good thing.

IMAGINING A BETTER FUTURE FOR OURSELVES IS NOT FANTASY

We can believe God for many things, but the one thing that holds us back is our failure to imagine a better future than the one we have already got. Because, let's face it, it is easier to live in the darkness of temporal doubt than in the light of eternal hope.

Without renewed minds, our formula for survival is to go for damage limitation, which stops us going forward to a 'promised land' while convincing ourselves that staying in Egypt is better. It is an enslaved way of thinking, which has us living with a false expectation of nothing really changing. But, of course, it does – we will just regress further in our lives while a little bit more of us dies inside.

If you are not someone of faith and have no concept of God's love for you, most of what the Bible says will sound impossibly hopeful. And I get it, but think for a moment: What if you could put aside your own logic and resist redacting those chunks of the Bible you have historically struggled with and begin to imagine some of it might be true? What do you think could change in you? What do you think it might do to your world-view?

The twentieth-century German theoretical physicist, Albert Einstein, reportedly said, 'Logic will get you from A to B. Imagination will take you everywhere else.'

Leaps of imagination have led to innovations in science, technology, mathematics, philosophy, astronomy, physics, industry and medicine. The amount of accelerated change in the last fifty years has been staggering. It feels as though we have gone from bicycle to space rocket in hardly any time at all.

So let's just stop and pause for a moment on how we have been given the extraordinary power to imagine and innovate a future through faith and works. What is more, that comes with no boundaries, no borders, no restrictions or compromises. A faith fuelled by love and driven by the belief that God knows exactly what he is doing.

It means not being frightened of change. The real threat to our progress does not come from what is outside of our control, but what we control and repress within.

Albert Einstein says: 'When I examine myself and my methods of thought, I come to the conclusion that the gift of fantasy has meant more to me than any talent for abstract, positive thinking.'[13]

And this is a rational, logical, scientific thinker talking.

God has granted each one of us the gift of being able to think for ourselves. As Paul the apostle reminds us, 'There are different kinds of gifts, but the same Spirit distributes them.'[14] It means our lives will look different to each other, because we have different needs and situations, while sharing the same loving attention from the Giver of aspirations.

NOT JUST OUR IMAGINATION

Will you file your dreams away under 'interesting, but never going to happen' or will you draw upon them as a spiritual direction to help shake and transform society? Because, for one, I am pretty sure they will play a key part in how we will reach all peoples on earth. As Joel prophesied: 'In the last days, God says, I will pour out my Spirit on all people. Your sons and daughters will prophesy, your young men will see visions, and your old men will dream dreams.'[15]

Along with the logical and practically minded, we need more, not fewer prophets, dreamers and visionaries to see a reformed culture built around God's hope for the world. The Spirit of God rests on each one of us to lead others into their own stories of rebirth, not through secular stories of fantasy with its own version of positive thinking and moral truth. It needs to come through the Way, Truth, and Life – Jesus Christ.

The interruptions we seek are our requests and petitions to God to recalibrate our lives and reset our minds to point us towards a better, more superior way to exist, as with Jacob, Joseph, Joshua and everyone else who had a vision to believe in more.

The imagination is the port from which to set sail to discover new lands of promised blessings and opportunities. To dream the impossible and release the improbable. To see God's glory fill the four corners of the earth.

Just think about this before we move on to the next chapter.

This could be your time to dream new dreams, to revisit old dreams, and imagine the transformation in your community you have always longed to see but dared not believe. And if you are someone like me who doesn't usually dream or at least remember them, all it just takes is one simple bedtime prayer before you close your eyes.

As Jesus said, 'Everything is possible for one who believes.'

May all our hearts respond, 'I do believe; help me overcome my unbelief!'[16]

Sleep well!

INTERRUPTER

YOUR LIFE IN THE FUTURE

Take time to imagine what life might look like in five years' time. Let your imagination go, I dare you!

Picture what you see yourself doing. Where you will be living. Where you will be working. What family life looks like. If married, what your relationship looks like. If a church leader, what your ministry looks like.

Do you like what you see? Does it fill you with a sense of faith or fear?

Or do you see hope with a fresh start, a new beginning with opportunities never before experienced?

What do you need to get there?

Do you need help to believe to overcome your unbelief?

Using your imagination, begin to see everything with God is possible . . . and then pray into it. It might just happen! It might not, but to begin is half the task. Be bold!

6 HOW TO BE AN EVERYDAY ORDINARY HERO

Okay, here is my confession.

Back in the day, my teenage years were disrupted by the sound of Punk and New Wave, so I did what a fanzine at the time proposed and learnt three chords and formed a band.

At the time I wanted to be like Ian McCulloch, the singer of Echo and the Bunnymen. Obsessing over his cool image just as much as the music, I hoped in some kind of fantastical way that some of his allure and charisma might rub off onto me. I learnt that the singer backcombed his hair with Coca-Cola to make it stand up, which was fine until summer came along and it became a meeting point for single wasps.

Now at the risk of sounding like I have famous friends (I don't), one evening my friend Dave invited me to a small benefit gig organised by an anti-heroin charity. Behind it was legendary guitarist of The Who, Pete Townshend. He had just started to work at his sound studios. As I watched a new band from Manchester perform their first London gig, Pete Townshend came and stood by me. Seeing an opportunity, I cheekily said, 'Buy us a pint, Pete!'

Five minutes later I was elbowed and a cold beer was placed into my hand. He asked for my thoughts on this new band called The Stone Roses, shared what he was doing and asked if I had any plans to tour. He even

> **I CAN DO THIS ALL DAY!"**
> CAPTAIN AMERICA

> **I CAN DO ALL THIS THROUGH HIM WHO GIVES ME STRENGTH."**
> PAUL THE APOSTLE[1]

offered me a lift home in his car, but I had to decline as I had my mum's old Renault 12 parked just around the corner.

Dave rang me early Monday morning, hardly able to contain himself with laughter and said, 'You never guess what? Pete thought you were Robert Smith of the Cure!' I was hurt, not because Pete turned out to be mistaken, but because he didn't think I looked anything like Ian McCulloch.

One of the problems we face at different points in our lives is how we relate to ourselves and others to be able to know how best to get on in the situation we find ourselves in.

WILL THE REAL YOU STAND UP?

Many of those in the public eye will say from time to time they struggle with Imposter Syndrome, a mental state where you feel inadequate, doubt your abilities, and believe yourself to be an absolute charlatan. It particularly affects those who have tasted success or been in leadership.

Because here's the thing, the more known we are, whether it is in church, education, business, sport or entertainment, the harder it can be to live with our accomplishments. So much so that on our worst days we don't feel we deserve anyone's praise at all.

It makes me think of the psalmist's words, declaring the greatness of God out of their own self-awareness: 'I praise you because I am fearfully and wonderfully made; your works are wonderful, I know that full well.'[2]

God is exalted and praised for the complexity of creation and is acknowledged as the author of every detail of our being. Derek Kidner says these original Hebrew words can be translated as 'For all the mysteries I thank you; for the wonder of myself, for the wonder of your works.'[3]

I know, the thought that you could call yourself 'wonderful' just feels laughable, doesn't it?

But if you are stuck on issues of how you see yourself and how others might see you, the chances are you are going to have a problem in how you relate to God, even though he has made you and knows you right down to your shoe size and preferred notch on your belt.

How to be an Everyday Ordinary Hero   73

It is why we look to role models to help compensate for what we think is missing in us. Pastors may look up to a leader with a large church and a profile on Instagram. For a business entrepreneur, it might be Elon Musk or Jeff Bezos, but if our thoughts are left uninterrupted, we run the danger of projecting this false graven image of ourselves onto others.

Meanwhile our confidence to be our true self slides increasingly away from us until one day we forget who we really are and how to be ourselves. What is more, our story becomes all about the person who has never been enough. And that is tragic.

POSITIVE ROLE MODELS

So let's talk, because I believe that God wants to heal the burden of self-falsehood to restore the true you. Where do we start finding answers that lead to a closer relationship with a supernatural, super-loving God who surpasses all human understanding?

Cultural commentator Grant Morrison says that comic book super-heroes help fill the void left by 'a culture starved of optimistic images'.[4] He argues that these latex-suited heroes fit with who we want to become tomorrow, given half the chance. There is a desire for power where all our best qualities are strong enough to overcome the disruptive forces that want to stop us in our tracks.

In the Marvel Cinematic Universe, there is often a dark side to their characters, such as with Hawkeye, but there is eventually enough self-awareness, and willingness, to see redemption and forgiveness. Where we find voids in ourselves, we can look for them to be filled with another person's story.

We live in the stories we tell ourselves. In a secular, scientific rational culture lacking in any convincing spiritual leadership, superhero stories speak loudly and boldly to our greatest fears, deepest longings, and highest aspirations. They're not afraid to be hopeful, not embarrassed to be optimistic, and utterly fearless in the dark.

They're about as far from social realism as you can get, but the best superhero stories deal directly with mythic elements of human experience that we can all relate to, in ways that are imaginative, profound, funny, and provocative. They exist to solve problems of all kinds and can always be counted on to find a way to save the day. At their best, they help us to confront and resolve even the deepest existential crises. We should listen to what they have to tell us.[5]

The thing all superheroes have in common is that their lives have been interrupted in a way that makes it impossible for them to live as they did before. Ignorance may have been seen once as innocence, but 'with great power comes great responsibility', to coin a phrase from our friendly neighbourhood Spider-Man.

Paul the apostle says to the church in Ephesus that they now know what they know and there is no going back. They are now enlightened and should go on to make better decisions. 'For you were once darkness, but now you are light in the Lord. Live as children of light.'[6]

Everything that is illuminated in our own life has the potential to become a light to others. But it all starts with our lives needing to be interrupted – and often by something that cannot easily be ignored or pacified by avoidance.

Spider-Man saw his uncle murdered because he chose not to get involved in a seemingly unconnected mugging.

Iron Man came to regret his inventions of advanced weapons of mass destruction when they were eventually used and turned on him.

Batman was born into a privileged family, saw his parents gunned down by a psychopath which then led him into a lifetime's crusade to protect society from evil villains.

And so on.

But here is the one other thing they all have in common – they all become a form of saviour to the world.

And we are attracted to saviours.

The origin of 'saviour of the world' came from a Roman idea and was a title given to its emperors. It gave a moral justification for occupation, expansion of their empire and suppression of whole nations. However, *Pax Romana* (Roman Peace), effective as it was for trade and travel, operated through fear and cruelty. What is more, there could be only one saviour for it to work: the emperor.

This was why the angels' words to the shepherds at the time of Jesus' birth were so incendiary to their first-century hearers. It was the language of sedition. 'Today in the town of David a Saviour has been born to you; he is the Messiah, the Lord.'[7]

They were not just sweet words spoken by a child with cardboard wings at the school nativity, but were dangerous, even outrageous

How to be an Everyday Ordinary Hero   75

words that declared war on injustice and oppression. The fact that the angels also mentioned the birthplace of Israel's greatest king only added to Jesus' calling card.

In God the Father sending his one and only Son, a new saviour comes to free a world from fear and oppression, sin and shame. But it's even more than that, Jesus gives us a new system for doing life through a relationship with himself, which includes renewing the mind and reforming society. And, unlike *Pax Romana*, this will see all people prosper, regardless of position and privilege.

It is in us to want to see someone save the day.

We want someone to rescue the princess, to defeat the Death Star, to restore the kingdom and banish evil to the outlands for ever.

O SUPERMAN

Have you ever thought how very dull superhero films would be if there were no interruptions? But, of course, the same can be said of everything. All film and TV drama exists because something breaks into the continuity of someone's life. Something interrupts the status quo and forces them to make an unplanned response. In the same way, if our superheroes faced no jeopardy, what would be the point of their existence? We would probably all want our money back!

If our superheroes did not see the upset as a challenge to reset, nothing would change in them or in the lives of others around them. No one would need to be saved.

Back in the nineteenth century, the philosopher Friedrich Nietzsche developed the theory of *Übermensch*, which translates as Over-man or Beyond-Man. We know it more commonly as 'Superman'. He declares, 'Behold, I bring you the Superman! The Superman is the meaning of the earth. Let your will say: The Superman shall be the meaning of the earth!'[8]

Nietzsche argued that the God-Man should be replaced by Man-God, so we can become the master of our own destiny. Only then can we have freedom and reach our full potential as human beings. It is a view that has become popular over the years, with many people pursuing it as alternative to putting their faith in Jesus. Of course, we might simply want to call it 'individualism'.

76   Life, Interrupted

It is also at odds with a faith in Jesus that believes through weakness
we become strong, through pain we can still triumph, through dying
to ourselves we can be raised to new life. In fact, with anything that
represents the kingdom of God in thought, word and deed.

But this all seems unnecessarily like hard work, not least when the
onus is all on us to make life a success – whatever success looks
like. Also, I am not sure someone born in poverty with no access to
clean sanitation, education or basic human rights would agree! How
this picture contrasts with Paul's words to the church in Corinth: 'My
grace is sufficient for you, for my power is made perfect in weakness.
Therefore I will boast all the more gladly about my weaknesses, so
that Christ's power may rest on me. That is why, for Christ's sake, I
delight in weaknesses, in insults, in hardships, in persecutions, in
difficulties. For when I am weak, then I am strong.'[9]

Unfortunately for Nietzsche, his ideas on superior human thinking were
largely rejected after he unwittingly fuelled Nazi ideology in the 1920s,
which saw the emergence of a German super race – a self-elected elite
group who believed that they could advance the world in their own image.
A place where the weak and imperfect had no place or right to coexist.

This is not a totally new idea. Aristotle, the ancient Greek philosopher
and scientist, thought all congenitally deformed children should be
killed at birth. We might say today that this showed diminished responsibility, but he was of a mind that said let's leave it to the gods to
pick them up if they so wish, not our problem. It was not until Rome
was Christianised in the fourth century under Constantine that infan-
ticide was made illegal, but the problem with humanity remained –
the myth of superiority.

How different Marvel's Superman is from Nietzsche's Superman.

If you are a comic geek, you might have already considered the similarities between Superman and Jesus. Although you could easily see
our caped hero as much like a Moses or Elijah figure.

Superman was created in the days of the Great Depression in America
in the 1930s. There was the Wall Street Crash and with it came wide
unemployment, poverty and hunger, but there is always someone to
profit from someone else's misery. The underworld, organised crime,
began to seize power in the shadows.

Today it is still hard to comprehend how a comic character could
speak hope into the harsh economic climate of 1930s America,
which saw so many people lose their life savings, jobs and homes.

BIBLICAL PARALLELS

It makes Superman's story sound almost biblical – and that's no accident.

Superman was born on the planet Krypton, the one and only son of parents Jor-El and Lara and was named Kal-El. *El* is the Hebrew word for God. As a baby, his parents, making the ultimate sacrifice, send Kal-El to planet Earth in a small spaceship just moments before Krypton is destroyed. Much like Moses hidden in a basket, he is hurried off to avoid death or a life of slavery.

His ship lands in the American Midwest countryside, near the fictional town of Smallville, an unimportant backwater of a place. Much like Nazareth.

Like Pharoah's daughter finding Moses, Kal-El is adopted by farmers Jonathan and Martha Kent, who name him Clark. The original comic book names for his adopted parents were Joseph and Mary.

As he grows up, Clark becomes aware of his various superhuman abilities, such as incredible strength and impervious skin. His parents advise him to use his abilities for the benefit of humanity, and so he decides to fight crime.

He is clever, brave, powerful, influential, but he also has that faraway, other-worldly look about him, while managing to blend in perfectly with the company of others.

When in action he wears a skin-tight outfit in patriotic red and blue with a red cape; the cape signifying kingship.

Superman's enemy is a villain called Lex Luthor, a name not unsimilar to Lucifer, who is fuelled by a desire for power and control over humanity and who wants to seek power and glory for himself.

When Superman is off duty, he is a photographer for a newspaper called the *Daily Planet* in the fictious city of Metropolis. His normal appearance as bespectacled Clark Kent is underwhelming. We are in on the secret that he is fully alien with the appearance of being fully human, but without this dual life his character would have nothing like the same appeal to us.

In Clark Kent we see an imperfect, stumbling, shy human being who condescends to our own human experiences, including his small nuisances, petty difficulties, minor frustrations – and awkwardness in relationships. In fact, probably much like you and me.

In 1965 Jules Feiffer wrote what is considered to be the first critical history of the comic book superheroes of the late 1930s and early 1940s, and suggests the main appeal of Superman is 'in the concept of his alter-ego . . . Kent was not Superman's true identity . . . just the opposite. Clark Kent was the fiction . . . Superman had only to wake up in the morning to be Superman.'[10]

We see someone who uses his outward appearance to reveal his inner character. He does not use a distant, Greek-godlike fame to win the heart of newspaper colleague Lois Lane, but is someone who shows a vulnerability to be able to be personally known and to show much as he loves her. He is both fully other-worldly and fully human.

It is the in-built need in us that wants to applaud ordinary heroes, as with the 100-year-old, retired British soldier, Captain Tom Moore, who raised an incredible £33 million for the NHS during the Covid-19 pandemic by walking laps of his garden. He became known to the world as the humble old soldier who inspired us to think no one is helpless to make a difference. His hope-filled saying, 'Tomorrow will be a good day', infected us all to be positive about future life.

SUPER HAIR-BRAINED THINKING

One of my favourite ordinary Bible heroes is Samson. It is not out of place to call him an eleventh-century BC superhero. And, as with Elizabeth and Zechariah, it starts with a mother who can't have a child.

> The angel of the LORD appeared to her and said, 'You are barren and childless, but you are going to become pregnant and give birth to a son. Now see to it that you drink no wine or other fermented drink and that you do not eat anything unclean. You will become pregnant and have a son whose head is never to be touched by a razor because the boy is to be a Nazirite, dedicated to God from the womb. He will take the lead in delivering Israel from the hands of the Philistines.'[11]

Unlike Zechariah, Manoah the husband had no problem imagining having a son; he just couldn't imagine how he was going to bring him up. But God had a plan. Furthermore, he was going to raise a saviour for the people, someone to take on the formidable and fearsome Philistines. Oh, and he was also going to have a superpower – given to him through his long Nazirite hair.

But as we know already, like Spidey – with great power comes great responsibility.

How to be an Everyday Ordinary Hero   79

Samson grows up and is told that as long as he lives within the limits of the Nazirite lifestyle everything will be okay. We read that 'He grew and the LORD blessed him, and the Spirit of the LORD began to stir in him while he was in Maheneh Dan between Zorah and Eshtaol.'[12]

However, Samson has a weakness for the ladies. It was his Kryptonite. His perfect life is interrupted by a less than straightforward marriage, which doesn't end particularly well.

Later Samson unleashes his superpower in Gaza as he rips off the vast doors of the city gate before carrying them to the top of the hill to make his escape.

But it is meeting the woman from the Valley of Sorek that is his interruption to doing God's will. And not in a good way.

Delilah agrees for a large sum of money to be a 'honey trap' for the Philistines to defeat Israel by Samson's downfall. All she needs to do is discover the secret of his strength. So after three attempts and with Judge Samson being worn down by her constant complaining, he folds and tells Delilah about his super hair.

The rest isn't pretty. His long hair is cut, his eyes are gouged out and he is thrown into prison before being sentenced to death.

One of the saddest things we hear about in the church is the fall of leaders. Richard Foster wrote how there are three great temptations for our age – money, sex and power – and says we must treat each one with respect and not underestimate their ability to control our every thought and action.[13]

These three things are not the preserve of church leaders. We can all get seduced by attention which feeds the ego. As Richard Rohr comments: 'It is sadly true that most institutions and nations admire and reward sins of the "spirit," and various forms of arrogance and greed often lead to promotions and praise. But pride, ambition, and vanity are still pride, ambition, and vanity; they do not stop being capital sins because someone is pope or president.'[14]

Samson allowed the interruption of a bad thought to enter his mind to shame his body, but the story finishes on a note of redemption. He repents and God restores his strength, although not his sight, to bring down the enemy by collapsing the two large supporting pillars of the building he is standing in. We're told that Samson 'killed many more when he died than while he lived.'[15]

80   *Life, Interrupted*

It is hard not to see an allusion to Jesus on the cross. The Saviour of the world is flanked by a thief on each side of him. He says about himself: 'Unless a grain of wheat falls to the ground and dies, it remains only a single seed. But if it dies, it produces many seeds.'[16] This is the Saviour of you and me, the real Saviour of the world who, unlike Samson and all the Roman emperors, was sinless and was able to achieve more in his death and resurrection than in his whole time on earth as a human being.

By the way, have you ever wondered what the 'S' on Superman's chest stands for? Maybe you thought it stood for 'Superman'. Well, it did until the 1978 film when it became known as the Kryptonian symbol for hope, an emblem for the House of El, the family of Superman. Superman reflects Jesus not just as the Saviour of the world, but the hope of the world too.

BE YOURSELF, EVERYONE ELSE COULD BE MISTAKEN

Advent is a time when we traditionally interrupt the wintery season with its dark nights and cold days to celebrate hope and light coming into the world. After Jesus heals a man with a deformed hand in a synagogue on the Sabbath, he turns around to the crowd and quotes Isaiah's prophecy about being the fulfilment of an ancient promise, which sees a loving Father sending his Son into the world to proclaim justice to the nations. He says, 'In his name the nations will put their hope.'[17]

You will have figured out by now that superheroes and followers of Jesus share some things in common: it requires courage to stand apart from the contrasting views of others. It requires self-sacrifice. It requires resilience made increasingly stronger through the determination to press on through adversity. It requires a loneliness when you feel in that moment everything depends on you. And yet, you will still do it. Why?

I would like to think it goes well beyond simply an obedient calling to follow Jesus. It is because we enjoy our life in him, we have found our purpose and its rewards outweigh the reasons to quit. We know it draws us closer to God's heart, into his presence, the very place our heart longs to be.

Whatever it is we are feeling today, our call is first and foremost to be living examples of God's grace. To be human, and not to try to be superhuman in what we try and achieve.

Our superpower is knowing that we are loved and forgiven by Jesus and out of that place his presence will flow into every area of our lives and into the lives of others through us, even those we will struggle to love. Because at the heart of it is a wonderful reassurance, as Julian of Norwich reminds us: 'The place which Jesus takes in our soul he will nevermore vacate, for in us is his home of homes, and it is the greatest delight for him to dwell there . . . And the soul who thus contemplates is made like [the One] who is contemplated.'[18]

While you think about what it is to live in the House of El, ask yourself how much of what you do is shaped by you trying to be someone that no one asked you to be. Have you ever let the following perceptions wound you?

- Have you ever been offended when no one thanks you for working an extra-long week?
- Does it ever bother you that no one notices that you hardly ever make time for yourself?
- Do you ever imagine how much your hard efforts and commitment would be missed if you weren't there doing what you do for others?
- Are you hurt by the lack of praise that someone else would get if they were doing what you do?

Now consider the public Jesus and the private Jesus.

What do you see in him and how his attitude differs to yours? Maybe take a little time to pray before moving on.

BE YOURSELF, EVERYONE ELSE IS TAKEN

When starting out in church ministry I confess that I took some of my strategic thinking more from the business world than from the ministry style of Paul. This was partly because I had come from the business world, so it felt familiar to me. Besides, we all need mentors, right?

Although I was trusting God, I felt an outward pressure to make progress, but I noticed how easy it was on those days when confidence is low or exhaustion hits to borrow from the 'fruit stall' of another leader. Borrowing their notes is one thing, borrowing their character is quite another.

It is not a good place to be in, because you also end up taking a short cut to hearing God speak to you, which is why I like the advice: be yourself because everyone else is taken. Besides, as the late singer of Nirvana, Kurt Cobain, is thought to have said, 'Wanting to be someone else is a waste of the person you are.'

This of course, is a question of authenticity.

We want to be ourselves and love in a way that we want to be loved. Not for what we do, and with all our imperfections on show. The late evangelist Billy Graham reportedly said that 'When wealth is lost, nothing is lost; when health is lost, something is lost; when character is lost, all is lost.'[19] I used to say to newcomers at church that our family was made up of imperfect people, so you'll fit in just fine. You could often feel the sigh of relief straightaway!

Being the real you might seem scary because you feel more comfortable hiding behind a shield of pretence but, as Eugene Peterson says, 'If I, for a moment, accept my culture's definition of me, I am rendered harmless.'[20] We are not always sure people will accept us for who we are without having a good story behind us.

Robert (not his real name) came to our church and, like most newcomers, sat at the back. He told me after the service he was there only because he was checking it out for a friend. He told me he was a Christian but then ended up coming along for himself and eventually gave his life to Jesus and was baptised. But Robert had started his journey of faith by cloaking himself in another identity as he felt his own true self would reveal a neediness.

The interruption I needed for my own life was perversely Covid-19. My mental strength, work rate and ability to multitask in several areas was not the superpower I thought it was. Looking back, it was hubris – and, let's face it, super-stupid. How often our so-called humility and 'works of service' are cloaked in 'Christianisms', rather than Christ.

But the good news is, like Samson, the Lord will redeem screw-ups!

GOD TAKES OUR WEAKNESS TO MAKE IT HIS SUPERPOWER

The truth is, the kingdom of God will never have to depend on you alone to get the work done. Why? Because we are all a work in progress and it will take a village to raise a child. I have said at various times to leaders over the years that it is not about getting the job done, but getting the person finished. It is about discipleship, not craftsmanship. It is about seeing beauty bloom amidst the toughest, roughest soils through kindness, acceptance and unmerited grace and generosity.

We may not feel especially gifted and know that our character has flaws, but we are all loved by the Father just as we are. But it is not something to go to our heads, just to our hearts – and for it dwell deeply there.

Because it is only in the interruptions of our best intentions that we have the opportunity to reflect and be restored by the one 'Saviour of the world', the One who wears a crown of thorns.

In the meantime, we have an ongoing task to learn to become more aware of the internal and external relationships to our soul, along with the spiritual battle between good and evil. And this is where interruptions save us, as Blaise Pascal observes: 'Is it not clear that man has two forms of consciousness, two levels of existence? If man had never been corrupted, he would enjoy perfect truth and happiness. But equally, if he had never known corruption, he could not be aware of that truth and happiness – for we know things by experiencing their absence.'[21]

Each interruption can begin to save us from ourselves. For myself, the interruption on a Scottish mountainside was about the need to demolish the idol of 'how great I am' to sing 'How Great Thou Art'. It was a gracious and loving invitation by Jesus to put an end to poor self-awareness and to come down a mountain of my own making.

There can be room for only one *Ego eimi* – I am.

It is why it is so important we get this, not least for those in a privileged position to influence others, which can be any of us.

If our western culture lacks having spiritual awareness, it is only in the same way that a fish lacks knowing it lives in the ocean. Because God's presence is everywhere. We just need to be reminded of it sometimes – and sometimes it will need an interruption to do it.

Meanwhile, we can choose to live each day with wonder.

We are more than equipped by the Holy Spirit to share our love for others, just as we are, along with our unfinished character, wearing the ordinary clothes of a follower of Christ, while powering up with all the resources under heaven to see his kingdom come – the one true superpower.

In humility and honesty, we can bring the thunderbolt of meaning and significance to a world longing for a true saviour by simply being us.

This is our true superpower.

To eternity and beyond.

INTERRUPTER

WHAT ARE YOUR REAL STRENGTHS AND WEAKNESSES?

Write down five of your personal strengths followed by five of your personal weaknesses.

Which ones took you longer to write?

Because we tend to be achievement-driven and always looking for acknowledgement, we will naturally want to draw our strengths from where we have had success or, as Arthur Brookes suggests, where we have more of something than others. Equally, we will draw our weaknesses from where we have failed or by seeing that we have less success than others.[22]

Now ask yourself: Which strengths and weaknesses are most likely to be used by God to reach others?

What does that tell you about your strengths and weaknesses?

⑦ MAY I STOP YOU RIGHT THERE?

I had hit a tough time.

It was the worst national recession for several years and as a result I had become an unemployed advertising executive. I cannot begin to say how much of a huge interruption it was to my carefully choreographed career, which I had been planning since my last year at art college.

I had thought this was going to be a blip, but it was not to be. I had signed up to all the specialist recruitment agencies in London, but I was either under-qualified or unqualified for the few jobs they had.

The thought that Jesus had a better plan hadn't really sunk in.

Fortunately, my Ford Whatever-It-Was car was safe from repossession. I had had the foresight to tick a box on the form, which covered me for fire, theft, illness and . . . redundancy. Never has a small square tick box meant so much.

Beyond income, I had lost my daily routine. My weeks became emptier than a dustbin at a national waste disposal conference.

My big plan was to wait for the recession to blow over, but nine months on and there was little change in my prospects.

> **FOR IT IS FROM YOU, O GOD, THAT ALL GOOD THINGS COME. FROM MY GOD COMES ALL THAT MAKES ME WHOLE."**
> ST AUGUSTINE OF HIPPO[1]

> **BUILD UP, BUILD UP, PREPARE THE ROAD! REMOVE THE OBSTACLES OUT OF THE WAY OF MY PEOPLE."**
> ISAIAH 57:14

But something started to happen in this period of interruption. I started to pray like I had never prayed before.

I read Jesus' words, 'Seek first his kingdom and his righteousness, and all these things shall be given to you.'[2]

I initially thought maybe this is how you get what you want from God. You give him something and he gives you back what you need. It felt like a good arrangement to me.

Over the following days, the Holy Spirit kept these words in the forefront of my mind. I meditated on them and slowly began to trust the promise, but my prayers didn't quite go where I planned them to. I was still trying to control the outcome.

I started to think: What if my future happiness starts with a set of new priorities?

What if I started to seek Jesus above everything else as opposed to simply first seeking out a career job every day?

I considered how I prayed and when I prayed. To my surprise, it wasn't half as much as I had thought. At this point, I don't think I had ever been to a regular prayer meeting. There had always been something to do or a place to be.

I considered how I worshipped and when I worshipped. Again, it wasn't half as much as I had thought.

But I comforted myself that I served weekly on the church worship team, so a big thumbs up there. Although, in truth, this was not so much of a sacrifice as me fancying the worship leader who incidentally later became my wife.

I considered my giving to God. Again, it wasn't half as much as I thought. I often gave what was left each month, which it will come as no surprise wasn't a great deal – or much of a sacrifice.

It began to dawn on me that I didn't feel rich in either my wallet or in my spirit.

So I came up with a clever plan. Between Monday and Friday at the start and end of each day I would do a prayer walk around the common behind the house. And if nothing else came from it, I would at least have killed two hours of time.

May I Stop You Right There? 89

Days became weeks and weeks became months. It got to the point where I looked forward to 'prayer walking'. I even extended my time on occasions to walk further.

But I still had some way to go to get anywhere near the desert father, Abba Isidore the priest, a monk of Scetis, who said, 'When I was younger and remained in my cell I set no limit to prayer; the night was for me as much the time of prayer as the day.'[3]

Almost without knowing it I was learning to be in communion with God. In these times I found I was developing a habit of gratitude and would be constantly sharing good and anxious thoughts, money fears, rent worries, dreams and aspirations, and my feelings for the worship leader, of course. I was learning to surrender myself to God and giving him permission to transform me by his grace as I started to see his mercy upon me.

I noticed, too, those attitudes towards having a glittering advertising career were starting to change in me.

By the autumn, something quite unexpected happened. I felt God started speaking to me about going to theological college and training for church ministry.

This was not in my game plan, but I began to pray about it with a small number of trusted friends, hoping their wisdom and first-hand knowledge of me would quicky confirm that I was an idiot for thinking it and put me off, but for some strange reason they didn't.

Meantime, I was told of a job going with a Christian charity who needed a copywriter and was encouraged by my pastor to go for it. It was not a job I was particularly interested in and I thought it was a big step down, but somehow I squared it with myself that it would serve me until I could go off to college in the following autumn.

As you can see, my life was not so transformed by grace as I might have thought at this time.

To my surprise the charity offered me the job.

But then I got a phone call.

It became the interruption to the interruption.

An advertising recruitment specialist told me that I had been offered an opportunity to work at one of London's top advertising agencies.

90   *Life, Interrupted*

After months of disappointment, I could not pretend to feel unmoved by the prospect. The only problem was my promise to God. On top of that I had to let both the charity and the agency know by the end of the week if I was going to accept their job offers.

I was thrown into turmoil, and not a little distraught. My shadow self wanted to renege on my promise to God. I mean, this was Saatchi & Saatchi. Most people would sell their grandmother to work there. Both sets of grandparents, if it helped.

I can honestly say that this was my toughest Friday ever.

I revisited Jesus' words about seeking first the kingdom of God, and went for an extended prayer walk around the common. He reminded me how he promises to add things, not just take them away. I tried to get his words to fit my desire for the advertising job, but the more I tried the more I felt like the ugly sister trying to squeeze her size 12 into a glass slipper.

At 4 p.m. I was ready to make the call.

'Hi, I am really sorry, but I am going to have to say "no" to the job.'

'What?' came the shocked reply.

'Um, yes, I am going off to theological college to train to be a church pastor.'

'You don't turn down a job at Saatchi's', said back the raised voice.

But I did. I put down the phone. I felt sick in the pit of my stomach and as if I was on anything but a roll, but I quickly made the call to the charity before I could back out.

It was only at the point of my action that I began to experience anything like the peace described by Paul the apostle – 'the peace that surpasses all understanding'.[4]

St John Chrysostom suggests that 'happiness can only be achieved by looking inward and learning to enjoy whatever life has and this requires transforming greed into gratitude'.

This kind of transformation was needed in me. Although I had begun to see clearly how God had set a course for my life, I struggled with gratitude. It was not the path that I would have planned for myself, but I was learning that a joyful, fulfilling life is never best realised by

May I Stop You Right There?　　　91

having life on your own terms. It starts with gratitude at having the privilege of following Jesus and not with the desire for things you would have at any cost.

One of the most important lessons I have had to learn as a follower of the Way over the years is that Jesus doesn't seem to care half as much about our career paths as we do.

He cares so deeply about us not to leave us alone that he will bring interruptions to get our attention. Think about it. If he didn't love us, he would just let us go our own way – uninterrupted, uninhibited in whatever direction we wanted.

We will often hear the well-meaning saying that as one door closes another one opens. I have yet to find that verse in my Bible. Instead, Scripture is full of stories of two doors being open. It is full of ordinary people being called to walk God's way, but it always comes with choice.

We get to exercise the God-given gift of free will and choose which way we want to go. And with it there will either be jubilation or sadness in heaven. We can choose the path of either gratitude or greed.

Guidance takes as much perspiration as it needs inspiration. Or is that just me?

It is a journey of discovery. It is often hard work. It can challenge every inch of us with what we believe – or don't.

We may want that light-bulb moment or quick fix, but so often the slow-down feels like a put-down, but this is to misunderstand God's loving nature. It is in the quietness, when we can't see much happening, that the shepherd's voice is often heard the loudest.

My place of quiet lasted for months, but it was by the stillness felt through reflection and meditation that I began to be drawn into new, unexpected, heartwarming experiences of God's love for me. I got to see another side of him.

I did not see a radio DJ with a prayer request show, but a heavenly Father who actually liked spending time with his child and who had removed all the clocks in the house to prove it.

The psalmist says, 'He leads us by still waters.'[5] We are not pushed into places where we must go and then told why we must be grateful. Neither will he ever manipulate a situation.

92   *Life, Interrupted*

This is why I think the Lord graciously left two doors open for me, as painful as it was. He wanted me to know that I still had a choice and control over my life. To have only had one door might have led to some resentment in me later.

Even in times of great interruption we still have a choice how we will respond.

And we begin to choose by learning to seek first his kingdom, not our own kingdom. We courageously lay down our agenda, whether it is needing a job, our marriage being fixed or an answer to a big life question.

The things that get added unto us aren't like those things on our Amazon wish list. They are better, eternal and blessed in every way.

We have seen that a God who forces his will on us is not a loving deity, but a coercive, dictatorial one. Healthier thinking is to reject the Christian fatalistic view of one door closing. Sometimes we are clearly meant to pray for doors to be open. This was the experience of a young Dutch pastor called Brother Andrew who wrote: 'Our prayers can go where we cannot . . . there are no borders, no prison walls, no doors that are closed to us when we pray.'[6]

He refused to accept what he called 'the heresy of Christian fatalism', which said if a door is closed it must be God's will. As a result, millions of Bibles were smuggled in behind the Iron Curtain to the persecuted underground church in the old Soviet Union, as well as later to many other closed or dangerous parts of the world.

There was a famous advertisement in 1970s America taken out by the Episcopal Church to warn of the danger of religious cults that said, 'Christ died to take away our sins, not our minds.' It told us to use our heads with our hearts. How much easier it is, though, for someone to tell us what to do and where to go without us needing to question anything. How easy it is to want to have our relationship with God in the same way.

This is not to be confused with us being obedient to his will and with the things he has entrusted us to carry out in his name. But godly guidance is always a close collaboration between the heart, mind and soul and Father, Son and Holy Spirit.

Maybe there is an inherent spiritual laziness in us that looks for short cuts. Anything that removes the effort and won't slow us down.

Maybe we want black-and-white answers because we want life to have simple rules and to be easily understood, but we all know how grey the area of ethics can be.

For instance, when is a war a 'just war' and when is it about ideological domination? Or when is it right to turn off a life machine? Or when do you tell a sick person bad news that could kill them? Isn't it easier to simply keep it hidden?

We start in prayer but need to take the step of faith to believe our heart and mind will work in synchronicity with the Spirit of God that will lead us towards the experience of James, the brother of Jesus: 'Wisdom that comes from heaven is first of all pure; then peace-loving, considerate, submissive, full of mercy and good fruit, impartial and sincere.'[7]

God is doing more behind our backs than he is showing to our faces. His agenda is not our agenda. His timing is not our timing.

SAINTS NEED NOT APPLY

Pope Francis made a rare appearance on an Italian TV chat show with an even rarer admittance for a pope: 'I am not much of a saint.' He said that, when he was a child, he had wanted to become a butcher. That is quite a change of direction in life![8]

And maybe this is where God most likes to interrupt us. As I set out in the previous chapter, it is in those places of ambition where we have made our own plans the centre-point of our life.

The son of a pushy but well-meaning mum called Monica is remembered as a great Christian thinker and man of honest prayer. Aurelius Augustine, the highly educated, upper-class son of a Christian mother and pagan father (at least until his deathbed) had his career path set out for him, but his personal life would read like a sex scandal in today's tabloid newspapers and might even get a trigger warning at some universities.

As a bright young man, full of promise and ambition, he had a long-standing sexual relationship with an unmarried woman, but 'the real sin', at least to Monica, was that the woman was simply not good enough for her son.

He had a promising career as an elite scholar in Carthage and Monica was keen to see him mix in the right circles and flourish in life, so his mother asked him to break off his relationship. She then arranged for another young girl to be his respectable, well-connected future wife but, while waiting for her to come of age, everyone turned a blind eye as Augustine took a mistress to satisfy his libido.

But his story, although colourful, is not so much about his complicated relationships as a lust for human success at any cost.

By the way, I forgot to mention he was also a Christian at this point.

Martin Laird says, 'Unbridled careerism was the knot of Augustine's sin and sorrow more than his much more interesting sex-life.'[9] Augustine was to write later: 'My aim was to become an outstanding public speaker. My motive was sheer self-glory.'[10]

Augustine went on to become an eloquent voice to the Emperor of Rome, which he later came to regret and described himself as 'a purveyor of lies'.

On the outside he could be seen as successful, but inside his life was a mess. It was not that Augustine did not believe in Jesus, he was just searching for him in all the wrong places.

I suspect that is not much different from many of us who struggle with ambition and recognition, but somehow get misled along the way by those things that make us human – self-gratification and greed. Even though as followers of Jesus we are expected to know better. As Jeremiah eloquently puts it: 'From the least to the greatest, all are greedy for gain; prophets and priests alike, all practise deceit.'[11]

You and I wouldn't perhaps single out Augustine as an ideal candidate for church leadership, but God sees what we don't. It was the interruption of an elderly bishop looking for his successor that helped change the focus to Augustine's unhappy self-centred lifestyle, which became his saving grace. As a result, the young Augustine veered off his career path for a life that led to selfless service to Jesus.

This interruption saw Augustine embark on a beautiful journey of discovery of a God he never knew personally in his younger years, a God who never condemned him or left him, and loved him for who he was, regardless of some poor choices and twisted thinking.

His honesty, not least with his struggles of lust, culminated in a deeply personal autobiography that we know as his *Confessions*,

May I Stop You Right There? 95

which I think can be best described as one long, profoundly touching love letter between him and a merciful and loving God.

As the Bishop of Hippo, Augustine wrote candidly about his previous motivations:

My soul listen!

Do not let the din of your ego

deafen the ears of your heart.

The Word himself calls you,

He bids you to return to him.

In him is the place where peace abides,

Peace that is never disturbed.

It is the place where he will never forsake your love,

Unless you withhold your love from him.[12]

FINDING YOUR HAPPINESS AND CONTENTMENT

Jesus is in Judea and continuing his journey to Jerusalem when he is interrupted by a man of some local importance. Maybe he had heard Jesus' speech to the Pharisees on faith and fidelity and saw something refreshingly different about him, compared to the other rabbis but, whatever it was, he thought it was worth stopping Jesus to have a conversation.

Jesus allows himself to be interrupted even though, on the surface, the mission ahead looks more important than this one person. And here it is not hard to think about Jesus' parable of the one lost sheep and leaving the ninety-nine behind to find it.

The man says, 'Good teacher, what must I do to inherit eternal life?'[13]

If you had been in the Judean crowd, I guarantee you would have thought, 'Duh! What a dumb question! Every schoolchild knows the answer to that one.'

The man would have grown up knowing the Torah well inside and out. He would have been taught that keeping all the Ten Commandments was the answer to his question – and yet something within him cried out for more than head knowledge and to be affirmed in his faith by this rabbi.

Jesus' response is so beautiful, and it simply undoes me every time I read it: 'Jesus looked at him and loved him.'[14]

Jesus looks at him and loves him before he asks for anything. He is simply loved for who he is. It is as if Jesus says, 'You are so loved, why would I not want to stop for you?'

James Edwards suggests that 'perhaps he senses that the question of the man's lips is not the question of his heart.'[15] Whatever Jesus is thinking, it has the look of compassion on a lost sheep needing to be found by its shepherd.

We know through the help of Luke and Matthew's accounts that the man is a rich young boss of others, but of what or who we don't know. Yet Jesus does not look at the person as a man burdened with hypocrisy or arrogance, but simply like any one of us.

The Greek word for 'looked at' is *emblepein*. It is an intensified compound of the normal word for 'look', which means Jesus looked at him intently, even perhaps intimately, much like a father looks at his son when he comes with a difficult request that demands kindness and understanding.

But the big takeaway here is that Jesus sees him and loves him.

Occasionally I might bump into a young adult who used to come to church. They will see me in a café or on the street and come across and say 'hello'. They may tell me what they are now doing, but also of the not-so-good things, along with some of the challenges they are facing. But behind the talk I will see that look in their eyes and that question they asked as a young teenager: What must I do to get eternal life?

They are not bad young people. In fact, they are often more well-balanced than some older adults I know. And asked about Jesus, they will say that they still believe and pray.

Being a pastor, everything inside me wants to respond with love – even when some of their lifestyle choices and personal decisions might be poorly considered and are causing others pain.

These young people seem to have everything going for them. They have age, health, dreams and ambition. And yet nothing. They are concerned about global warming, wars, famine, disease and the state of humanity. They don't possess peace or purpose. They are

May I Stop You Right There?   97

anxious, keen to put society right, but can't quite figure out why they can't put themselves right. And it breaks my heart.

The rich young ruler had his life mapped out, he had financial security, he had years on his side and yet is a confused soul who is searching for satisfaction. He doesn't just ask the good teacher how he can inherit eternal life but falls to his knees before asking his question. There is brokenness and humility in his body language.

On the outside he is already doing well, but quite evidently on the inside there is an emotional crisis causing him anxiety and distress.

Frederick Buechner says there comes a time when you realise that living on salary and status alone is not enough. There is always the temptation to believe that we have all the time in the world. But a day will come when we no longer have life enough left to go back and start all over again. Buechner advises instead that 'we should go where we most need to go and where we are most needed'.[16]

But in the first place what we need to do, he says, is to listen to the voice of our own gladness, the thing that gives us the most peace. It will help leave us with the strongest sense of sailing true north, and of peace.

And when we find that gladness within, it is then about going where we could be most used, where we can make a difference to people's lives, which are marked by hard toil, grief, emptiness, fear and pain. It is about bringing to others the same gladness that leads to a life of contentment and joy. But it all starts with finding our gladness first.

Imagine how the rich young man's crisis of identity is hiked up even further when told by Jesus that if he really wants to know the answer, he must give everything he has to the poor.

He had maybe exhausted all other sources to help him find rest for his soul and now had come as a final resort to interrupt Jesus' journey to Jerusalem – the very man he was starting to believe could give him what his heart most desired. But the interrupter becomes the interrupted with a seemingly impossible challenge to give up everything.

It is not that wealth is a bad thing. After all, the wealthy woman we read about just a little later in Mark's Gospel, the one with the alabaster jar of expensive perfume, is not criticised for having money. Neither is Joseph of Arimathea who, as a prominent member of the Council, would have been considered wealthy.

BROKEN DREAMS

The question is all about: Who you will make the centre-point in your life: yourself or Jesus? Because one will bring joy and satisfaction, while the other risks bringing a lifetime of lost opportunities, robbing the heart of what it aches for and desires the most. And once those years are spent, there is no getting them back.

As a young church planter, I remember being in a room of pastors and seeing an older pastor sitting at the back. He told me how he was struggling with broken dreams, at which point my heart broke for him.

All through his many years of ministry he had believed that God was going to make his church a big city church, but it was just one knock-back after another. There had been prophetic words spoken over him and the church but now, as he faced retirement, he realised it was not going to happen. And it hurt. Really hurt.

I can't confess that I had any great insight in that moment, so we just prayed, and the Holy Spirit graciously ministered to this precious man, but his words stuck with me and made me ask: What does inheritance from God really look like? Is it something seen or something more hidden, profoundly unfathomable, soulful and eternal?

It is easy and maybe a little bit lazy to simply write off the rich young ruler for being the victim of a privileged lifestyle, but my heart goes out to him more than just a little. And if you feel sad for him too, good news! You are becoming more like Jesus. You see him and you love him, regardless of his wealth, position, lifestyle choices or poor decisions.

The young ruler had kept the Ten Commandments and did exactly what was asked of him, but ultimately, like Augustine, it led to inner conflict.

This story continues to be an interruption two thousand years later. It rightly disturbs us with a divine affection, requiring a surrender of the soul for all who thirst after truth; a spanner in the works of those thoughts that search for purpose and meaning in all the wrong places.

Our gladness, our joy, come by seeking first the kingdom of God, the sweetest of all surrenders, which will see joy and peace flourish in us, along with new ambitions for the soul.

May I Stop You Right There?

This is our real treasure, our gold, our fortune in waiting, our security and comfort because this we know: our relationship with money will always be an indicator for where our relationship is with God. It just is.

It takes no small amount of humility to have a real conversation with Jesus about how you are feeling today but, like the rich young ruler, don't expect it to be on your own terms.

Expect your life values and everything you hold dear to be interrupted to see the breakthrough in your life you need but are yet to know.

Learn not to expect cosy, comfortable responses when you pray. Hard as they are, take these times as signs of God's affection and overwhelming love for you. And if they put you out, remember, they could be the things that put you right.

KNOWING YOUR MIND TO HEAL THE HEART

1. How do you feel about some of your attitudes towards others being interrupted by God?

2. What do you know that is hidden away in you? Is it envy, resentment, pride, criticism or something else?

3. Do you allow it to flavour your conversations with others, albeit subtly?

4. You might not like to hear it, but character always gives itself away. 'For there is nothing hidden that will not be disclosed, and nothing concealed that will not be known or brought out into the open.'[17] So why not begin to be open to change?

5. Naming it out loud will help loosen its grip on you. Sharing with others will help 'move the dial'. Surrendering it will help God's light overcome the darkness.

8 TO BE CONTINUED . . .

When I was small, I loved watching the old TV show, *Batman*. It featured Adam West, nylon tights and some rather hammy acting. I am not sure anyone would argue that time has not been kind, but to these young eyes it was thrilling. However, the one thing that always ground my beans were the three words that would pop up at the end of some episodes . . . 'To be continued . . .'

It was a killer! I would have to wait a week, another 168 hours, before knowing if Batman and Robin would escape from a vat of poisonous chemicals as the clock ticked down to zero. Of course, you knew they always would.

All good TV drama series, and especially soaps, like to operate with 'cliff-hangers' because the writers know it is the way to keep us invested in their characters and what happens to them. By the end of each episode, interest has piqued, imaginations have been fired and senses entertained. But we need to have a conclusion of the experience. In other words, we need satisfaction.

David Hillman and Adam Phillips point out, 'We use interruption when we have a sense of a completable process. Only something with an assumed (or already known) beginning, middle and end can be interrupted.'[2]

I have found that an interruption affects me only if it has created a feeling in me that wants to continue with the experience that has gone on before. Perversely, too, I have found it can be the very thing that is used to make me more invested than I would have been otherwise.

"

TAKING A NEW STEP, UTTERING A NEW WORD IS WHAT THEY FEAR MOST."
FYODOR DOSTOEVSKY[1]

"

GOD IS LIGHT; IN HIM THERE IS NO DARKNESS AT ALL."
1 JOHN 1:5

102   *Life, Interrupted*

This is what a good cliff-hanger will do; it interrupts us to make us care more about what has gone before and gives it a greater value. It is why we get feelings of frustration, anxiety, sadness or anger – we have suddenly felt the loss of something.

It is why we resent it when watching weekly TV episodes and a commercial break suddenly pops up. It makes us want to opt for more ad-free streaming services such as Netflix and Prime. We know there we can binge-watch without any interruption. But are we better for watching back-to-back, one-hour episodes without a break? I am not so sure.

Could it be, then, that God allows interruptions to help make us more appreciative of what we already have and to make what has gone before more valuable to us – making us more grateful?

FAMILY VALUES

One of my favourite stories of restored families is that of Joseph and his brothers. His family were rich compared to most others around them. Jacob, the father, had proved himself to be an astute businessman when he had successfully negotiated an equity partnership with his uncle Laban. He began to do incredibly well for himself: 'In this way the man grew exceedingly prosperous and came to own large flocks, and female and male servants, and camels and donkeys.'[3]

The Lord continued to bless Jacob with children. To onlookers they appeared to have everything, but all families can have their secrets. And this one had a pretty dark one!

Joseph was just seventeen years old when his jealous brothers sold him into slavery and then told their father how he had been devoured by a vicious wild animal. In the years that followed the family did their best to carry on. Meanwhile, they grew richer, not least with seven amazingly good years of back-to-back harvests. But then the good times were over, and a famine threatened to leave them all destitute.

This became the disruption to help restore and heal their family.

An older Joseph reveals himself as their saviour, the Lord of Egypt, and as still being alive to gobsmacked brothers. Eventually Jacob makes his own way down to Egypt to see his long-lost son and the stage is set for an emotional reunion.

The story concludes with the family being financially richer than they were before the disruption. However, the real richness comes with a family restored and being even more valued than before. It completes what was not appreciated before. As Jacob says to Joseph: 'Now I am ready to die, since I have seen for myself that you are still alive.'[4]

It is not hard to see how Joseph's life foreshadows Jesus' life. It is a similar story of rejection and the raising up of a saviour who offers complete forgiveness and new life for the broken hearted. As the famine was a necessary interrupter to see God's will done it also helps point us neatly towards seeing why Jesus' coming was so necessary.

THE GREAT DISRUPTER

I hope you are beginning to get excited by how Jesus's life, death and resurrection are the greatest disruptions the world has known!

We see how Jesus is born at a time of global hardship and oppression with a mission to repair the broken relationship between Creator and creation, which has been corrupted by sin – redeemed only through the sacrifice of himself.

From a twenty-first-century perspective, Good Friday looks like a form of cliff-hanger in the story of Jesus' life and ministry, but at the time many people – believers and non-believers alike – thought that was it. There was nothing to be continued. Everything had ended.

There was completion, but then no completion, because there was no satisfaction. Everything was left high and dry.

But as the next three days tell us, the story was not finished.

We see the tables turned and, far from being a momentary interruption to the continuity of the world's trajectory, something profound has just happened and with it comes an earth-shattering revelation: Jesus is not just an interrupter of life, but also the Disrupter of death.

It helps makes sense of his words in John's Gospel: 'I have come that they may have life, and have it to the full.'[5]

Jesus is about the continuity of life, but it gets even better still. It now comes not just with forgiveness of sins, but also with the gift of eternal life, which is made possible through the death and resurrection of Jesus.

As a disruption it is something that is permanent and can't be undone or reset to how things were before. As Jesus says from the cross, 'It is finished!'[6] It means death has lost its grip on us and is no longer able to hold humanity to ransom with fear, shame, and suffering.

Sin is cancelled, not the person.

Now, seriously, that has got to be worth an 'Amen!'

Jesus as the Great Disrupter wonderfully fulfils God's plan for us, which in Bible-speak is called faithfulness. The Son is the centre point of time, not a touch point in history. In himself, he completes the story and gives a beginning, middle and end.

To make sense of Jesus disrupting death, we need to go all the way back to the first ever interruption. 'In the beginning God created the heavens and the earth. Now the earth was formless and empty, darkness was over the surface of the deep, and the Spirit of God was hovering over the waters.'[7]

From the very first words of Genesis, we see how formless, uninterrupted chaos is subdued by God, who takes a decisive action of compassion and speaks into the silence of non-existence. As a result, the continuity of nothing – meaninglessness – is once and for all broken. The darkness is shattered with the gift of the world's first dawn. But it is what happens next that we easily miss.

NAMING THE DARKNESS

God names darkness as 'night' and presents it within the cycle of each day, which is constantly interrupted by the light – as if almost to show who is boss!

It is the daily reminder, and a point for continual praise, of the permanency of God's action to disrupt the darkness that welcomes in the light of the world.

Each new dawn is a powerful symbol of God's continued presence in the world and shows just how much he is in control – and that he is for us. It is a constant reminder of the promise that the darkness will never silence us again.

The writer of Lamentations puts it so well: 'Because of the LORD's great love we are not consumed, for his compassions never fail. They are new every morning; great is your faithfulness.'[8]

Right back in Genesis with the disruption of light on the first day we see how the scene is set for Jesus' coming. The gospel-writer, John, makes the point brilliantly in his prologue: 'The light shines in the darkness, and the darkness has not overcome it.'[9]

God speaks light into the meaningless, lifeless, nothingness of what has gone before and continues to speak the permanency of the Word – Jesus.

This is a real 'drop the mic' moment, and John's first-century readers' jaws would have been heard falling one by one to the floor. It remains for me one of the most powerful ways ever to start a book. The continuity of non-existence has been permanently broken by God with the continuity of existence.

STORIES OF CHANGE

Most ancient cultures have creation stories, which tell their own versions of the origins of the cosmos and their own interruption. I have found that all of them here have similarities because all recognise that something had to happen first to move the story on, although it must be said the Big Bang theory doesn't allow for interruption because you can't interrupt infinity.

As we see, a definition of disruption is an interruption which brings a permanent change and has a permanent consequence. It is more than a blip.

Interruptions can be said to be like punctuation in a sentence, like this one, which help to control reading breaks to give the narrative continuity, clarity, meaning and greater definition. We could say this about the way God acts in history. He continues to interrupt life paths to steer the whole of humanity towards truth. Jesus perfectly punctuates and completes God's plan to bring his healing and hope into a broken and fallen world.

Genesis shows us that nothing can happen without interruption.

The story of salvation begins with three words, 'in the beginning'. They become part of a sentence which leads to a narrative to form a book. And like all good books, it has a clear beginning, middle and an end.

When I read the accounts of stories that interrupt ordinary individual's lives in the Bible, I see that they are far from random. They are used

106   *Life, Interrupted*

to punctuate the purposes of God. Each moment, like a comma, is intentionally placed, along with every one of God's words and actions.

In Jesus' genealogy at the beginning of Matthew's Gospel, the characters are like commas, semicolons, full stops and paragraphs. Through a timeline of forty-two generations over two thousand years, each one carries God's original purpose to save all of humanity.

CHANGE IS HERE TO STAY

I used to say with frequency in my last two churches, 'Change is here to stay.' So much so that some people would actually finish my sentence out loud in meetings. (Well, it is good to know you're heard!) We were intentionally consistent with our language, and this was particularly important when we first planted the church.

Sometimes people came and sat in our living-room and told us how much they wanted to be in a small organic church and how they were done with organised big churches. We said the church won't always be twelve people. They would nod and agree, but we have found time and again that change always exposes character.

I suspect that not many people like change, unless you are my wife, but it is a fact of life. And where there is change, we tend to want to be the ones controlling it. No wonder then that most of the time we would prefer things to stay as they are and resist anything that looks as though it might expect anything from us.

But have you noticed that, unless change is sometimes forced, how nothing much can change? Something often needs to happen to us to get our lives moving.

Donald Miller says that as people we will 'always seek comfort and order . . . even if comfort isn't always that comfortable'.[10] Not least when we may secretly be hoping for something better to come along.

When my children were small, we used to love watching *Oliver Twist* (the musical), but I never found it easy watching Nancy's story unfold. As the girlfriend and accomplice of the despicable Bill Sykes, she was violently abused but stayed loyal to him, making it emotionally difficult to live her life. She even called it love. Beyond Charles Dickens' grim characterisation of nineteenth-century domestic abuse, it is still the reality for many women today.

Some will say, 'Better the devil you know', meaning that the familiarity of relationships, however broken or abusive, is better than an unfamiliar future, which might turn out to be worse.

Just the thought of changing anything for fear of making life worse becomes a powerful reason to stay put. Everything is rationalised. The situation may be terrible but justified because at least life is consistent and will come with no surprises. But at what cost? You may remember that it didn't end too well for poor Nancy.

BREAKING THE CYCLE OF FEAR

But this points to the one fundamental question facing all humanity: How do you break the cycle of suffering? Often, we use an expression, 'You can't make an omelette without breaking eggs' as a philosophical way to entertain changes, but unless the heart and mind are in it, we will quickly regress to maintain the status quo.

When I was around eight years old, my best friend at the time encouraged me to run away with him. We had both fallen out with our parents over something and thought we could do better for ourselves. A new life beckoned us, free from rules and punishment – and of course no bedtime routine. So we pumped some air in our bikes, bought a bag of sherbet lemons and set off.

However, after just over an hour, I was starting to think this was not such a good idea and worked out that if I turned back I wouldn't miss dinner and, more to the point, wouldn't get into trouble. My friend reluctantly agreed, but I could see huge disappointment in his eyes – even fear.

I didn't realise until much later and older how serious abuse at home was for my friend. His parents were ultra-religious and used to hit him and his older sister so hard they had scars on their bodies. They would try to disguise this when they went out. They would be locked in their rooms for maybe a couple of days, forced to miss meals, and to read their Bibles until they showed signs of repentance and contrition. It was heartbreaking.

Unless something forcibly interrupts our lives for some, I fear the story won't change. We all want to live our best lives, but it will always take courage for it to become a reality.

WHO WILL GO?

My working life has never been linear and at one point I had to return to the advertising world when we were struggling with our finances as a young family. By this time, I had become a creative director of a small busy ad agency in Covent Garden, London, working a good few hours a day.

However, call is call and it wasn't long before God started speaking to me about church planting. Something, I hasten to add, that I had promised to myself I would never, ever, ever do, partly because I thought you either had to be short of any common sense or it was only for people who couldn't get a proper job.

One of the ways God started to prepare me for church planting (which ended up being in East Anglia) was through the job itself.

One afternoon I was in my office reviewing a reel of TV ads for a charity called Samaritans when one commercial used a news montage of farmers standing by their dead livestock. It was at the time of foot-and-mouth disease, a terrible condition which affects cattle, sheep and pigs along with other animals. It had been discovered in an Essex abattoir in 2001 and had quickly spread across the country.

As I watched farm workers weep over lost livelihoods, something broke in me. I had never really had much affinity with the countryside beyond a couple of weeks each year in Devon, but this affected me deeply, so much so that I began to weep and had to quietly shut my office door.

As I continued to watch I began to hear a voice inside my head say, 'Who will go?'

'I don't know,' I mulled silently.

Again, I heard the voice say, 'Who will go?'

'I don't know!' But this time out loud.

Then for a third time, but louder, I heard the same voice say, '*Who* will go?'

'*I . . . don't . . . know!*'

The words stuck with me like one of those very annoying radio jingles for a phone store. I just couldn't get the question out of my head. After a while, I perceived, rather slowly, that maybe, just maybe, the Lord was speaking to me. What is more, I felt he was birthing in me an affinity with the countryside which, it must be said, to a west Londoner is no small thing!

It was one of many interruptions that would shape our plans for how we would eventually establish a semi-rural church.

When we finally arrived in Suffolk, we made contact with a rural charity that specialised in befriending farmers who suffer from mental illness, money worries and loneliness. For several years, we made it our priority to support them, particularly at harvest time.[11]

When God interrupts your life, it is likely he will also interrupt your values. The Spirit of God will want to shift your outlook, rearrange your values and priorities – and often all at the same time. He will want to mercifully deal with your fears and anxieties around the unfamiliar while bringing you encouragement to help you to transition into a new story of his making.

IT IS NOT JUST ABOUT YOU!

As we were to discover, it was not just an interruption to change our lives, but to interrupt a whole community to rewrite the stories of our neighbours, to become aware of God's great love for them. Over the years we prayed we would see interruptions become invitations and for people to welcome Jesus into their lives.

We will always want to resist change, so why wouldn't we expect God to keep breaking in? Why wouldn't we graciously see him encouraging us to move on to the next place that he has got in store for us?

Jonah's story sums up to me how I felt in the early days of being called – a bit of a reluctant messenger.

His book is nestled between two other minor prophets, Obadiah and Micah, in the Old Testament. I say book – but it is just two pages long. However, it is a big, big story so I think it deserves to be called a book. It starts with a prophet of the Lord who had chosen to live life on his terms, thinking he could get away without it having any consequences.

However, Jonah's world was interrupted with God's view of the world. The prophet had distanced himself and been operating from a place of familiarity to keep himself holy and pure. But this was all about to

110   *Life, Interrupted*

change. 'The word of the LORD came to Jonah son of Amittai: "Go to
the great city of Nineveh and preach against it, because its wicked-
ness has come up before me."'[12]

Nineveh was a flourishing Assyrian city and an important stopover for
commercial trade. Founded by a descendant from the line of Ham,
the son of Noah, it had become synonymous with sin.[13] But God's
words are too much for Jonah and he runs away in the opposite
direction and hops on a ship bound for Tarshish.

So God sends a storm that puts the lives of everyone on the ship in
danger. Knowing there is no escape, Jonah declares himself to be
the problem to the crew and passengers and they reluctantly throw
him overboard.

The storm stops, the sea calms and everyone on board at this point
puts down their sick bag.

We see that, after a lot of internal struggling, not least with the issues
of anger and self-righteousness, Jonah realises what Nineveh needs
the most. It is not another voice of judgement, but a voice of compassion. A voice that speaks words of life.

The 'called life' of a follower of Jesus is to give sight to the blind and to
denounce the darkness that obscures anyone from seeing Jesus as
the life-maker, not the life-breaker. C.S. Lewis puts it best: 'I believe
in Christianity as I believe the sun has risen, not only because I see
it but because by it, I see everything else.'[14]

When God breaks in and stops what we are doing, it is an invitation
to open our eyes and draw nearer to the centre of his presence.
Richard, the thirteenth-century Bishop of Chichester, prays:

> May we know you more clearly,
> love you more dearly,
> and follow you more nearly,
> day by day.[15]

With each new dawn that breaks out of the darkness of the night, the
Lord continues to make all things new. Each day is a fresh invitation
to renew our spirit and refresh our soul. To liberate the mind from the
tyranny of the lie that we can never change to believing that 'with God
all things are possible'.[16]

Freedom without fear is a good feeling, but without welcoming interruptions as invitations we may risk missing out what God is doing
in us. If you and I can start by first embracing that change is here to

stay, our next prayer might be to ask the Lord to give us courage to move on as he moves in us.

RUNNING THE RACE

We might have figured out by now how a change of circumstances will bring a change of perspective and with it, quite likely, a change in our character. It might even result in a change of pace of life and its securities. This was certainly the case with me when I got Covid-19 back at the beginning of the global pandemic, but the long interruption gave me the gift of time to deeply reflect that something had to stop and something else needed to start.

Since our sabbatical in 2018, I had had a creeping feeling that as a pastor of a growing church I could no longer do the job as well as I would have liked. Although it was necessary in the early years to get the church up by doing two jobs, there was an increasing problem. The church had become not just a bigger animal, but a different one. My capacity to work in two jobs was also reaching its limit. In truth, I was much nearer to breaking-point than I cared to acknowledge.

While away Emma and I had briefly talked to the Lord about the future and what it could mean for us, but on our return to the UK, things happened and we just had to hit the ground running and, well, we just kept running.

Eventually, we picked up the conversation with the Lord and we spoke to him about how we wanted to see more of the things that we had dreamt about all those years ago. We were hungry to see greater breakthroughs and transformations in those precious lives we had not yet met. However, we hadn't really thought through how it could mean putting ourselves out of a job to see it happen.

Here is my confession: if I had not become so ill with Covid-19, I would have found a way to bravely carry on. However, between you and me, I think it would have looked increasingly messy. Not just to me, but to my family and our beloved congregation. How hard it is to let go of our ego and remember the kingdom of God does not stand or fall all on our successes, gifting or long hours.

John Bunyan writes, 'It is my duty, said he, to distrust mine own ability, that I may have reliance on him that is stronger than all.'[17] This was what I was to experience in the many months of illness.

Paul the apostle talks famously about how the Christian life is like running a race and we should 'run in such a way as to get the prize'.[18] There are times too when 'calling' can be seen as a relay race which has others coming before and after us.

We could even say that there has only ever been one race, the same race, one that started back in the garden of Eden and has carried on all through human history with every generation of believers. But God is not in the grandstand; he runs with us, cheering us on, keeping pace with our every gasping breath and tired step, picking us up when we stumble and always pointing us to the finishing line.

Every book, chapter and verse in the Bible betrays his reasons for doing this. It is quite simply because he loves us. It is this purest of loves that spurs us on to the finishing line. In gratitude, 'We love because he first loved us.'[19]

The fourteenth-century English hermit, Richard Rolle, reminds us that our motivation for doing anything for God must have love at the centre of it, and not simply a love for doing it. 'If it is for God's sake that we love everything, we love God in it rather than the thing itself. And so we rejoice, not in it but in God – in whom, indeed, we shall glory and rejoice for ever . . . For God the Holy Trinity is to be loved for himself alone.'[20]

But while a race is a pilgrim's progress, there are many times when we need to stop, take a break and check if we are still in good shape to keep running the race without changes. If not, we should be grateful for the interruptions.

Each holy nudge, each correction, is like a punctuation mark and it is these pauses and breaks that give a spiritual rhythm to help us to prosper, not burn out, and to draw closer to the love of the Father.

Sometimes we will be required to lay down something we might enjoy doing or find our worth in. It might mean a complete change of direction. It will feel less like a comma and more like a full stop that leads to a new chapter. But the good news is that there is always more of God's story to be written over our life. As with Joseph and brothers, we do not fear it will be anything less than what we have received now.

We will become richer, not poorer for the interruption.

Because here is the thing: the book with our name in is not yet finished. There are plenty more blessings ahead. There is always a 'to be continued' message to be found at the end of each chapter of our lives. The author's ink won't run dry on us.

So let's just put a full stop here for you to be able to ask a couple of questions of yourself and pray before we turn the page.

INTERRUPTER

1. Have you got enough commas in your week?

   - What can you pause and interrupt this week to help you catch your breath?
   - Where does your private life with Jesus happen?
   - Do you have enough pauses for reflection and prayer?

2. What is currently exhausting you and needs a full stop?

   - Where do you need to stop and rest before you can continue?
   - Are you taking enough time off for yourself, and for your family to see you?
   - What do you think are the consequences if you don't stop?

Make a note of your answers, ponder over them and then pray.

Ask the Holy Spirit to guide your thinking and to punctuate your thoughts with some ideas of his own!

9 WET FEET

My wife and I planned to set off on a trip to the south of England to house-hunt. Being seasoned and reluctant travellers of the M25, the orbital motorway around London, aka Britain's largest carpark, we have learnt over the years to check the traffic before we leave the house.

I looked up Google Maps and Waze on my phone and both apps were telling us to go clockwise, so we duly followed the route intel. As we set off, we got into a deep conversation about something or other and, without thinking, automatically turned right to go on the M25, in an anticlockwise direction, which is the way I tend to go nine times out of ten.

However, still engrossed in our chat and not really paying attention to the satnav, we hadn't noticed until about thirty minutes later that we had gone completely the wrong way. By the time we had realised our error we were heading straight towards the heavy traffic – the one thing we were so desperate to avoid.

You might at some point have done something similar. Neuroscientists have a name for this – just to help us feel we are not going completely doolally. It is called Default Mode Network (DMN).

I heard a classical musician say that if they thought too much about where their fingers were on the instrument it would completely throw their performance. Wimbledon tennis men's champion, Andy Murray, has said that he plays at his best when he is not thinking.

> ❝
> WHETHER YOU TURN TO THE RIGHT OR TO THE LEFT, YOUR EARS WILL HEAR A VOICE BEHIND YOU, SAYING, 'THIS IS THE WAY; WALK IN IT.'"
> ISAIAH 30:21

'You're relying on instinct. That's why practice and repetition is extremely important.'[1]

I spoke to a junior pro at my local golf club who told me that he goes to the driving range most mornings at 8 a.m. and hits 500 balls. It is not that he is a bad golfer, far from it, he has won more than a few competitions – he just wants to get better.

Maybe you have switched off from what you have just read or not fully computed the last paragraph.

I am not offended and, if it makes you feel any better, our brains actually perform better and with greater accuracy when in DMN mode. Amazing, though, how the brain can still function in stand-by mode. A fact maybe to store up your sleeve for the future when you are berated by your spouse, boss or friend for not listening.

HOW DID WE GET HERE?

DMN has been called 'resting wakefulness'. However, none of this, of course, takes away that startling feeling of 'How on earth did I get here?'

This might be your experience now. You have just had a sudden realisation that things have moved on and you hadn't noticed.

There will be many periods in our lives where we may have switched off. I am not talking about the odd hour, but days, weeks, months . . . even years.

Life has continued, but then something has interrupted us. A switch has suddenly been flicked on and we find ourselves wondering, 'How did I get here? What did I miss?'

It is not always welcome, but it does serve a purpose.

It might be triggered by something as simple as looking at a box on a form where it asks for your date of birth and in that moment realising you are just months away from a significant birthday. It jolts you into thinking: 'How did that happen? How did I get here so quick?'

If you are blessed to be a parent, maybe your wake-up moment is the realisation that your small children are no longer, well, small. One of your children comes in and tells you there is an end-of-school prom, and your first reaction is, 'Whaaaaat!'

Wet Feet

It is in some of these wake-up points of my life that I have discovered what my life has become. It has also at times forced me to assess my relationship with others and God.

Recently my iPhone interrupted my day by throwing up a photo memory of my oldest daughter, Daisy. It instantly took me back to the time when she had turned eighteen. I had driven her to Stansted London airport to see her off to Bali for her to begin her gap-year experience. My camera caught the moment just as she went through the gate where she looked back at me with the biggest smile possible. It was a picture of sheer joy. I saw her newly found independence. And then I had a moment. I realised our relationship had changed.

I remember shedding a tear in the car as I drove out of the short-stay carpark. I was overwhelmed with a sense of loss and unexpected sadness, even though paradoxically I was immensely happy and proud of her decision to go off and see the world. Something that surely, deep down, a parent wants for their children.

I won't kid you, seeing the photograph on my phone all those years later reawakened the feelings of that day. I found myself pondering on the moment triggered by that smile. It made me more than just a little bit nostalgic for those younger years when my wife and I would bump into each other in the middle of the night with bloodshot eyes and half-awake awkwardness. I chuckled as I remembered how we would stumble into our young children's bedrooms every time we heard the faintest cry or whimper. Everything then was so new, so fragile, so scary and uncertain.

If you are anything like me, those years were plain exhausting. I would try and do my day job while struggling with sleep deprivation. Emma says for the first few years of parenthood she felt she was living in a constant haze but remembers, too, the day when it all changed, and she suddenly became aware that she no longer felt constantly tired.

But at the time it felt like an unending routine with constant nappy-changing, back-rubbing, burping and feeding – things we learnt to do with our eyes closed. Quite literally.

Even though there are times when life is a blur and each memory struggles to be recalled, it does not make any moment of the past any less meaningful or more unfruitful than the present; it just makes it different.

The writer of Lamentations speaks of the power of memory as a pathway into God's presence: 'This I call to mind, and therefore I have hope: The steadfast love of the LORD never ceases; his mercies never come to an end; they are new every morning; great is your faithfulness.'[2]

When I take time to recall the past and see where God has been present, it has a powerful way of releasing a desire of expectation for something else to happen in the future.

Celebrating a milestone well, whether it is the end of one phase of parenting, getting a promotion or buying your first home, helps to release the thing called gratitude to enable us to move forward into the next phase. But one thing I have learnt is that, however good it is to revisit the past, we are not called to relive it. Enjoyable as it was making sandcastles and eating ice lollies, neither Emma or I will miss the colic and endless broken nights' sleep.

However, not all memories are happy, and being prompted to look back only reintroduces us to a world of pain and confusion. We might also have made some poor relationship decisions and hurt the ones we loved. As Brother Lawrence observed: 'Thoughts spoil everything. All evil begins there. We must take care to set them aside as soon as we observe them not to be necessary for the task of the moment or for our salvation, so that we can begin again our converse with God, wherein is our only good.'[3]

BEING WILLING TO GET OUR FEET WET

When the Israelites arrived at the River Jordan, I am sure they were still carrying all sorts of baggage. Jordan was not Nirvana. Left behind in their trail was a catalogue of failures, embarrassments and missed opportunities. No one could argue that it hadn't been a tough but formative time in the wilderness. No question about it.

Now before them was a river that stood between them and their future. It was a place of transition, a planned interruption to the journey by God to prepare his people for what would come next.

You may have heard the desert experience used to describe death – physical and spiritual – but it was also a place of purification. I am sure God's people would have done anything to bypass the desert experience and go straight to 'Pass Go' and the promised land, but of course they would have been less prepared and in a worse mess later.

Wet Feet

Although the picture of the desert is of a place where death to old ways and to self is encountered, it also becomes the very place where they get to know themselves and figure how to have a relationship with God and one another.

Paradoxically, it is a place where they become alive by learning to live in God's presence. Alan Jones says, 'We don't go into the desert in order to wall up our heart. We go there in order to give it away, to God and the world.'[4] It is not a reclusive experience, but an inclusive invitation to bring life to others.

The early church fathers and mothers saw it as a place to gain wisdom, not to look foolish and small, which may explain why so many monasteries were founded in these largely inaccessible, desolate places. Not least as somewhere to go in the early days to escape persecution. In fact, they become places of rich encounters in God's presence. Many stayed in the desert!

Joshua was given the task of leading God's people into the promised land, but maybe it was not as far from the desert as we may think. Former Archbishop of Canterbury, Rowan Williams, observes how big the desert looks in photographs, but 'through the lens of faith we will experience it more as being the size of our own heart, mind, and imagination.'[5] It is as small or large as we want it to be, depending on the size of our desire and prayerful need to be alone with God.

Joshua, the leader of the free people, calls together priests of the twelve tribes and says each of them must go into the middle of the Jordan River, pick up a large stone and carry it out on their shoulders. Only then would the river become crossable for the ark of the covenant and allow God's people to cross safely to the other side.

But here was the tricky part.

The river was deep, fast-flowing and had underlying currents. To move from a place of death to new life meant getting your feet wet. There was no other route available and certainly no bridge or ferry. Only when they had taken the first steps into the river would they begin to see the water part for them to be able to reach the other side.

However, this is where memory is used as an encouragement to step out into the unknown. What's more, experience told them God could do it.

Moses had successfully led them across the Red Sea away from the tyrannic rule of Pharoah. And just like the forty years before, God was going to perform a similar miracle again.

While the first crossing was freedom from slavery, the second crossing would be freedom from death and slavery – something that wasn't lost on those who would be baptised by John in the same place some fourteen hundred years later. Some historians even think that Jesus' cousin may have baptised near the same spot the Israelites used to cross the water – just to bring home the point.

The interruption on the journey to the promised land by a deep river goes from being an obtrusion to an opportunity, a gateway into the fulfilment of God's plan for them.

The twelve stones were more than a souvenir or an achievement certificate for getting across the water and became a symbol of salvation. A sign of a promise being fulfilled as spoken long ago to Abraham and the patriarchs. The crossing would become a new memory to be stored up to give hope and confidence for the life that lay ahead. The meaning of the stones was very specific.

> Joshua set up at Gilgal the twelve stones they had taken out of the Jordan. He said to the Israelites, 'In the future when your descendants ask their parents, "What do these stones mean?" tell them, "Israel crossed the Jordan on dry ground." For the LORD your God dried up the Jordan before you until you had crossed over. The LORD your God did to the Jordan what he had done to the Red Sea when he dried it up before us until we had crossed over. He did this so that all the peoples of the earth might know that the hand of the LORD is powerful and so that you might always fear the LORD your God.'[6]

The stones become a reminder to bring comfort in knowing that God is always with us and always powerfully at work in our lives – whatever happens next. It means whatever comes along to distract us, knock us off course or cause us to stumble, the constancy of God's presence is a reassurance that he will always have the upper hand.

In fact, past interruptions can be the very things that God uses to help us to remain faithful for whatever happens next.

There were some embarrassing times in church services when I would be speaking and someone from the media team at the back would be waving frantically at me. My immediate internal response would invariably be, 'I am not stopping, I am on a roll!' Only for them to discreetly sidle up and turn my lapel microphone pack on. I am even embarrassed to say there were the odd times when I would go to the toilet and the team would need to thump on the door with equal persistence to tell me to turn it off!

Wet Feet 121

However, I think it is fair to say we find a way to learn to get through interruptions. But it seems to be God's way to use interruptions to continually remind us that change is at the heart of the Christian experience and is non-negotiable.

Probably at times we will all want to ponder what the future version of ourselves might look like, so casting more than a fleeting glance behind, along with a grateful heart, is not a bad place to start. It will give us encouragement to keep getting our feet wet to be able to see more of God's plan for our lives.

CHARACTER BEFORE GIFTING

Whatever the trigger is for waking up the soul from stand-by mode, it can do one of two things. It can either draw us into a place of reflection to prepare us for what comes next, or it can scare us into a place of retreat where we will inevitably find ingenious ways to avoid risk.

So let's talk character. And by character, I mean those things in our nature that form the pattern of our thinking and human behaviour.

At some point we may have switched off paying attention to how we behave because we don't like what we see in the mirror. It is not always because something has happened, but maybe because nothing has happened. The skewed way we may act, respond or relate to people, rightly or wrongly, has become so normalised in us that we are no longer aware of the slippery state of our soul.

When we are young, we start life wanting to change some things about ourselves while aspiring to change the world. Our motivations are likely to be both noble and flawed.

Maybe we want to change something in us to win someone's heart or seek recognition. Sometimes we will see breakthroughs, at other times we will fail, but this is how character is formed. It is built on the positive and negative experiences which then become a foundation for making all future decisions.

We naturally use our successes and failures as reference points for all our future aspirations, but this is also where our character partners with our dreams.

Our character is shaped by emotional experiences, so if we have suffered with envy or rejection, such as someone getting a job promotion over us, it will take root in us and begin to show up later in life, perhaps about our children's own achievements. It could mean that we never quite enter into joy for others because their success brings back painful memories.

What if we are in a 'sliding doors' scenario and got that promotion against all odds? We can take a different kind of problem into the future – imposter syndrome, a state of mind that leaves us anxious and constantly doubting our own ability. We know it shouldn't do but then we allow it to affect other areas of our lives, even our marriages and how we raise our children.

When intimacy or kindness is shown, our gut reaction may be to put ourselves down or withdraw to a place where we feel more comfortable, where we can live with less praise and need of affirmation. But what has happened before is more than a memory, it has become part of our character, of who we are – and unless we allow the Holy Spirit to break in it will leave us believing in less for ourselves.

The bottom line is that our character is made up of good and bad habits, which we could say are like muscles that need to be exercised. We will need them to help us make the best decisions. These 'muscles' give us a strength and confidence to move forward – and go the distance.

John Wimber, founder of the Vineyard Church movement, used to say all the time to us as leaders: 'Character before gifting.' This is not just about integrity in public life, but our private life, our solitary walks in the desert, our care for our own soul. As the writer of Proverbs reminds us, there is huge merit in self-examination: 'The purposes of a person's heart are deep waters, but one who has insight draws them out. Many claim to have unfailing love, but a faithful person who can find?'[7]

Developing a strong character gives us healthy emotional and spiritual wellbeing. It helps us to say 'no' when everyone around us says 'yes'. It means we can walk away when our ego wants to stay. It is why God will interrupt our plans to change wrong 'muscle memory', bad reactions, that make us act in a certain way in some situations.

As much as we may like, character cannot be developed in the quiet, unbroken places of life but only through the interruptions and uncertainties we face each day. Only in these times can the soul find the inspiration it needs to see the transformation it desires to see for itself.

Meanwhile, we must find ways to deal with those patterns in our behaviour that bother us. And don't think they don't get noticed by others.

A little while ago an old friend popped up on my Facebook feed. He had posted news about his new position as vicar of a church. The image of him triggered an old memory from some thirty years ago while at theological college.

I considered him a good friend, but he told someone else behind my back sometime later that I was arrogant. I was completely devastated by their withering assessment. Maybe it was pride, but it was not how I wanted to be remembered. Now I am not saying they were entirely wrong, I am just saying that is not how I want to be remembered.

It is no surprise, then, that when we get older many of us will find ways to accept our weaknesses rather than figure out how to change them. We might even feel tempted to downgrade arrogance as just over-confidence.

Over my years of pastoral ministry, I have seen how older people in churches are less likely to come forward for prayer than younger people. Sometimes I have noticed that their body language says, 'Nothing will change for me.'

It is built on an impoverished expectation to want to hunger or thirst for anything more. They have concluded that this is just how life is. There is also a hidden weariness for the things of God, which holds talk of spiritual renewal and outpourings at a distance from the heart. I have come to see this as the pain of grief speaking.

MIRRORS THAT DISTORT TRUTH

The mirror we hold up to see ourselves does not always reflect the image that others have of us. In fact, people can be more generous towards us than we are to ourselves. We really can be our harshest critic! The image we have of ourselves may still be the one left over from thirty days or thirty years ago. Like Dorian Gray's hidden picture in the attic, we would prefer others not to see the real us for fear of being rejected and unloved.

But here is the thing – God sees the whole picture. And if we struggle to show compassion to ourselves, it is likely we will struggle to show compassion to others. John the apostle says this 'is how we know that we belong to the truth and how we set our hearts at rest in his presence.'[8] Through the work of the Holy Spirit, kindness is multiplied.

What happens to us gets recycled and used again and again through our character and relationships with others. But here is the hope: 'If our hearts condemn us, we know that God is greater than our hearts, and he knows everything.'[9]

If we feel beaten, in pain, feeling frustrated or at a loss, Jesus is not done with us – ever. There is always a way for his final say in the matter. 'Dear friends, if our hearts do not condemn us, we have confidence before God and receive from him anything we ask, because we keep his commands and do what pleases him.'[10]

These commands are the spiritual disciplines that keep us fit and healthy in faith. It is about finding God in all things: in all memories, all circumstances, all moods and all outcomes. Margaret Hebblethwaite observes the problem of not taking the time to properly see ourselves.

> We frequently fail to make links of cause and effect that are literally apparent if we pay a bit of attention. We let ourselves be swirled on in life through a current of a mighty river: there is always a new call on our attention, a new distraction. We do not stop to look.[11]

We all need to discipline ourselves with the help of the Holy Spirit and create habits of self-awareness. This is the gift that prayer offers us by just being in Jesus' company.

I find ending each day in prayer before I close my eyes, and taking a little time to review my daily activities and reactions to situations, helps me to seek forgiveness from God and helps me forgive myself. Doing it at the end of each day helps to stop me building up 'compound interest' on unresolved feelings.

It enables my soul to be restored when it has been spent in the emotions of the day and gives me the confidence to wake up the next day to face new challenges. This is sometimes referred to as the examination of consciousness or, as Ignatian spirituality calls it, the prayer of examen.

Just one more thing to add: we need people. We will need to take a chance with trusting them with our story. It means, like the Israelites, we will need to get our feet wet to move on. Remember, we are created for relationship.

A small group of like-minded believers that meets mid-week in a home will gift us the space to be open and trusting of each other, a place to be vulnerable and known to each other. It will provide a mirror to help breach the gap between the person we think we are and the one seen by the people across the living-room. It just needs us to be real with God and real with one another.

Even though I might have winced at the old memory from theological college, I know that I am not the same person as I was then (and I am pretty sure it is the same for my friend) because God promises always to be at work in us, so we don't condemn ourselves with false pictures of ourselves.

You and I can choose not to walk through a grotesque hall of mirrors of our own making that wants to distort God's image in us. As Richard Rohr refers to Jesus' words, 'the lamp of the body will be filled with light': 'It is all a matter of learning how to see, and it takes much of our life to learn to see well and truthfully.'[12]

We can be filled with gratitude that the Holy Spirit is never done with us; 'the light of the world' will always find a way to shine through our earthen vessels to bring glory to himself. But it starts with an honest conversation.

In fact, former pastor and writer John Mark Comer uses a whole book to point out that the problem does not stop with telling lies to ourselves, but living them out in our attitudes towards others, ourselves and to God.[13] It reflects not how bad life is but how badly we are living it.

Maybe the best thing we can do now to begin to interrupt our wrong thinking is to learn to create the habit of a structured prayer life. I would like to suggest maybe trying the Ignatian prayer of examen. It doesn't take long, and it really doesn't matter when you do it in your day. Oh, and it is pretty easy to remember.

But at the end of the day, the choice remains ours in how we go forward.

Do we live uninterrupted with our patterns of behaviour tethered to past hurt, or do we have the courage to go one more time and set ourselves free to learn to love and be loved all over again?

But one thing is for sure, God is always greater than our hearts and his promise to us is that his love will always endure.

INTERRUPTER

PRAYER OF EXAMEN

I offer this version of an ancient prayer for you to use as and when. There is no time constraint, so pray as you can.

Get yourself comfortable.

Be still and quietly become aware of God's presence. Know that he is with you.

Pause.

Review your day with gratitude.

Pause.

How are you feeling right now? Do you need to make amends?

Pray for one thing that troubles you and hand it over to Jesus.

Pause.

Offer tomorrow as a gift to God and ask him to bless your sleep.

Sleep!

ADDITIONAL PRAYER RESOURCE

You may like to try using the free daily devotional resource **Lectio 365** from the 24-7 Prayer movement. It offers a space to slow down, meditate on God's Word and pray for 10 minutes at the beginning and end of each day. You can download it for free from the Apple and Android app stores.

🔟 YOU IN THE FUTURE

When we go on holiday, I am never that sure how much I need to pack, regardless of it being summer or winter. If you are used to going on holiday in drizzly England, you will share my dilemma.

My darling wife, on the other hand, having been steeped in the ways of YWAM,[2] has learnt to pack lightly, so much so that her clothes will fit into a small brown paper bag. Okay, maybe not that small, but her bag always goes neatly into the overhead locker on a plane. I can't pretend I am not a little envious, but even when experience is supposed to equip my thinking there are still plenty of ways to be caught out.

I had arranged to go 'wild camping' with a friend in the highlands of Scotland. I would be the first to say, I had become slightly obsessed with packing the right clothes, camping equipment and mosquito repellent along with a reliable torch. All those years of family holidays in Devon had taught me a thing or two. In fact, I had even trialled three types of light before we left.

We parked the car and headed into the Cairngorms where I began to walk with all the smugness of a happy camper with a PhD in outdoor savviness. By late afternoon, we stopped by the River Dee and began to set up camp. As we laid out the tent and poles, my friend asked me to hand him the tent pegs. The only problem was that there weren't any to hand him. Neither of us had checked to see if we had packed them. It was

> ❝
> **COME, THEN, LORD! WAKE US UP! CALL US BACK TO YOU! SET OUR HEARTS ON FIRE AND DRAW US TO YOU! BREATHE YOUR FRAGRANCE ON US AND LET US TASTE THE SWEETNESS OF YOUR PRESENCE! LET US LOVE YOU! LET US RUN TO YOU!"**
> AUGUSTINE[1]

> ❝
> **I KNOW, MY GOD, THAT YOU TEST THE HEART AND ARE PLEASED WITH INTEGRITY."**
> 1 CHRONICLES 29:17

a long silent walk back to the car – we had to then find a guest-house for the night.

You might have thought that by a certain age we would have enough experience behind us to see us through most of life's unexpected misadventures. But there is always something new to come along to disrupt our conceit. My experience in the Cairngorms became an experiment of how well we could get on for the rest of the holiday when our friendship was strained!

THE PLACE OF EXPERIENCE

In fact, the words 'experience' and 'experiment' share the same root word in Latin, *experior*, which means to gain knowledge through repeated trials. We often see the word 'trial' as something negative, something to get through or an ordeal. But it also means, more positively, repeated experiences to learn something of worth and of value. But what I have learnt too is that life will always give you the best experiences to experiment with how we put our faith into practice.

Our experiences are part of the 'survival equipment' we take with us when moving from one place to another in our lives. We will call on it at various times to help identify a solution to a problem. We will say to ourselves, 'I have been here before and this is what I learnt.' We call this wisdom.

It doesn't occur to us that the thing that interrupts us might not have been a problem if we had come to it with a different mindset.

Take this scenario.

Your boss stops what you are doing and calls you in for a meeting to chat about your job. You immediately go to the darkest place in your mind because experience has already informed you that you are going to be fired.

You make yourself ill with worry but enter the room ready to fight for your job. You have your game face on. Only your boss is not there to fire you but wants to offer you an assistant to take the pressure off you. Your experience of being fired has only happened to you once, albeit very painful, but you take that one time to think the worst for yourself and the worst of others.

You in the Future 129

We take this same pattern of response into other relationships. When a spouse struggles with something we have said or done we become defensive and look to put the blame elsewhere.

It can also cause friction in church when something needs to be said about how someone is coming across in a group or ministry-team situation. A person's insecurity and fear make it difficult for a reconciliatory conversation when often they are already preparing the ground to make themselves the victim.

But it is all a matter of perspective; so thinks C.S. Lewis, who says there is a clear difference between asking for forgiveness while really looking for a way to excuse ourselves in the name of forgiveness. So often we come to God not really wanting to confess our wrongdoing, but to elaborate on why he needs to accept our excuses for us to leave his presence unchanged. 'We are so very anxious to point these things out to God (and to ourselves) that we are apt to forget the really important thing; that is, the bit left over, the bit which excuses don't cover, the bit which is inexcusable but not, thank God, unforgiveable.'[3]

The starting point to change is not hard; it is believing that the impossible is very possible with God's help.

> Jesus asked the boy's father, 'How long has he been like this?'
>
> 'From childhood,' he answered. 'It has often thrown him into fire or water to kill him. But if you can do anything, take pity on us and help us.'
>
> '"If you can"?' said Jesus. 'Everything is possible for one who believes.'[4]

I looked up the word 'everything' in the dictionary and it means *everything*. It appears that there is nothing that cannot be fixed in us. The early church shows us they met and developed new ways of being, based on the trials of past experiences with Jesus. 'They devoted themselves to the apostles' teaching and to fellowship, to the breaking of bread and to prayer.'[5]

There were the regular gatherings in homes to take communion and pray together, but it was not just when it was convenient. They were learning a shared pattern of behaviour that would enable them to cope with all the many disruptions they experienced in preaching the gospel and 'making disciples of all nations'.[6] And it was always Christ-centred. 'Rejoice always, pray continually, give thanks in all circumstances; for this is God's will for you in Christ Jesus.'[7]

There was also the emerging pattern of regular encouragement among the early church to keep meeting, regardless of persecution and to be able to stand united in their faith and love for each other. 'Let us consider how we may spur one another on toward love and good deeds, not giving up meeting together, as some are in the habit of doing, but encouraging one another – and all the more as you see the Day approaching.'[8]

I suspect none of these new habits came so naturally that there weren't struggles when faced with fresh adversity and uncertainty. But something new was being birthed in them coming together and learning to have 'everything in common'.[9]

RESPECT YOUR SOUL

My family and I were driving back from the east coast of Scotland. Just before the trip we had bought a high-mileage, second-hand VW Sharan, which we nicknamed the Millennium Falcon. All of a sudden, the gearbox let out an ominously loud bang followed by a continuous knocking sound. I tried to ignore it at first, but we began to lose speed and the ability to accelerate. I discovered that shouting at it apparently doesn't help, apart from getting a withering look from my co-pilot.

Did I stop?

No! I just turned up the radio, tried to keep calm and carried on.

We crawled all the way home for five hours at 30 mph, annoying all the cars behind us. As I pulled into the drive the gears whirred crazily before everything came to a grinding halt. It cost nearly £2,000 to fix, which was more than the car was worth!

No one will ever thank you for just 'pushing on through'. It can be costly. You may think it is noble, but you are mistaken. It will only leave a trail of frustration.

We can't afford to ignore our soul's needs.

It requires us to be fussy and to not fill our souls with junk wisdom and ready-made social media advice. We need to find a better way to journey through life. Peter Scazzero calls this 'respecting your humanity'. If we ignore who we are as men and women made in the image of God, it will always result in destructive consequences.[10]

You in the Future   131

One day you may hear a 'clang' in your life; I hope you don't, but if you do, denial is not going to save you. It will only leave you crying on the hard shoulder saying, 'How did that happen?' Like all the best motoring advice, you need to do your health-check now, not later, to be able to stop a disruption turning into a destructive force.

YOU IN FIVE YEARS

Pastor Andy Stanley says if you want to know what you will look like in five years' time it will be an exaggeration of who you are now – unless something changes.

Look around.

Take a peek at an elderly relative or a friend you have known for years. Do you see them as someone with a different character from when they were younger, or are they a magnified version of their younger selves?

Are they being transformed by Jesus or are they living life the way they always have done, a life on their own terms? Now take a mirror and look at yourself. Do you like what you see looking back at you? Yes or no.

So what would it take to change? I mean really change. Inside and out. Who do you want looking back at you in the mirror in twenty or thirty years' time?

WE ARE ALL DISCIPLES OF SOMEONE

As believers we are all students of someone's teaching and influence, and who they are will matter as much as what they say.

Here's the thing, we will need to be prepared to see our parents, church leaders, teachers, politicians and police officers mess up. All falling short of the glory of God, much like us. But it is the mistakes of someone else, though, that teach us just as much how to behave through life.

We may like to think of ourselves as being our own person and free from someone's influence, but I think we both know it is a myth.

Someone will always be teaching us, whether it is a social media influencer or an unconventional rabbi from two thousand years ago. We

132   *Life, Interrupted*

are not the free-spirited, free thinking, free-wheeling, independently minded person that we think we are. There is always someone or something influencing our decisions to inform our human understanding and spirituality.

When we begin to follow Jesus, a transition is needed from old to new. 'You were told that your foolish desires will destroy you and that you must give up your old way of life with all its bad habits.'[11]

Paul warns how a sinful nature darkens the soul and is corrupted by deceit, which compels it to always look for new experiences to satisfy what is missing in a relationship with Jesus.

The role of the Holy Spirit interrupts all past experiences to be able to reveal to us a new experience. In the process he holds up a mirror and shows us what kind of fruit has been produced in our life while at the same time revealing a picture of our future selves and what it means to live a fulfilled life in Jesus. But it will need more than a teacher, it will need a counsellor and healer. 'Let the Spirit change your way of thinking and make you into a new person.'[12]

We will naturally want to compare ourselves to how we were before, but we also want to measure movement in our lives. We want the encouragement to know we have moved on and learnt something profound about Jesus' love for us and how it is transforming our view of the world and our place in it. Otherwise, we stay foolish and lost. To quote Proverbs, and forgive the picture, 'As a dog returns to its vomit, so fools repeat their folly.'[13]

BECOMING WISER

Spiritual transformation is as much about learning to be smart as it is encountering the holy, life-changing presence of Jesus in us.

His Spirit helps make us smarter, more informed, which means wiser decisions in our lifestyle choices and attitudes. But as writers like Richard Rohr, Henri Nouwen and St Augustine have said, the denial of having worldly influences leads only to a dual existence and in the end will frustrate and discourage us, so much so that we will wonder if any change is happening in us at all.

And there is a stark warning of the consequences of sowing from a place of dual living. James even calls it a friendship with the world that pits us against the love of God which makes us double-minded.

You in the Future   133

Paul says: 'A man reaps what he sows. Whoever sows to please their flesh, from the flesh will reap destruction; whoever sows to please the Spirit, from the Spirit will reap eternal life.'[14]

I am not sure anyone sets out to harvest a life sown from experiences where they have been indifferent or made poor choices. It is why the Holy Spirit puts a desire in us to help us see the future differently. And this couldn't be further than the western idea that we are our own person and all we have to do is to make our own future happen.

Here's what I know to be true: my good habits, which are patterned on the life of Jesus, are forged in me by the Holy Spirit. What is more, the more I invest in them the more they become exaggerated in me the older I get.

WAKING UP AND GETTING UP HAS NEVER BEEN EASY

Every so often I will bump my head on the wall during the night. My excuse is because from time to time I will need to spend a night away in a hotel or at a friend's house. It is made doubly worse by jet lag. The unfamiliarity of surroundings catches me out but, in the morning, waking up can be difficult. At which point I thank God for my phone's alarm sound.

Paul the apostle's words are a wake-up call that our future begins today, right now, not tomorrow. 'And do this, understanding the present time: the hour has already come for you to wake up from your slumber.'[15]

When we open our eyes first thing in the morning, if you are anything like me, it is usually not too long before a list of the day's activities starts to invade our thoughts. Some of these will come to us marked as urgent – and the battle to live in the moment and not to rush ahead in our minds becomes an immediate challenge. But has your soul woken up with you? Eugene Peterson's *The Message* puts it this way: 'Make sure that you don't get so absorbed and exhausted in taking care of all your day-by-day obligations that you lose track of the time and doze off, oblivious to God. The night is about over, dawn is about to break. Be up and awake to what God is doing!'[16]

The disciple and apostle, Peter, also sees the dangers of not paying attention too but adds a further warning. 'Stay alert! Watch out for your great enemy, the devil. He prowls around like a roaring lion, looking for someone to devour.'[17]

Every so often we get that 'wake up' moment where we realise we are not perhaps the master over all our motives, which is just as well as Jesus had no illusion about the hold that wrong patterns have over our daily lives anyway.

He saw how the long-term effects on people's physical, emotional and spiritual health could beat them down and cause hope to fade. Jesus saw the conflict between the person they wanted to be and the one they saw in the mirror: 'No one can serve two masters. Either you will hate the one and love the other, or you will be devoted to the one and despise the other. You cannot serve both God and Money.'[18]

Jesus disrupts the idea that you can have your cake and eat it and are able to live with the compromise of two kingdoms: God's and Satan's.

However willing the heart is, the head will always try and get us to go in the opposite direction. Like it or not, and uncomfortable as it is, there is a constant battle between the flesh and spirit within us that pulls us to the left and to the right with each choice we try to make.

There is no neutral ground or third way; our patterns learnt from experience will either make or break us.

WATCH AND LEARN

Jesus says to the disciples in the garden of Gethsemane, 'Watch and pray.'[19] In other words, be vigilant. Stay alert to the risks and dangers to the soul. Keep in close communion with the Father and he will help you win the raging battles within. This will be how you see the breakthroughs you want for yourself and for others.

This sounds like a full-time job to me, and it doesn't appear to come with holidays. Jesus knows that his instruction to 'watch and pray' is a key prayer strategy to help save us from ourselves and others' wrong influence. For our part it will mean we need to find ways to pay closer attention to what the Holy Spirit is currently doing in us.

We need to learn the habit of listening to the voice of love with an open mind and be obedient to the holy nudges. Well, you didn't think this would be easy, did you? St John Chrysostom said. 'Habit is a difficult thing, and it is hard to break and hard to avoid . . . Therefore, the more you understand the power of a habit, the more should you endeavour to be rid of a bad habit and change yourself over to a good one.'[20]

You in the Future 135

It is a discipline to get under the bonnet of the problem to really see what is going on inside of us. But this is done only by co-operating with the Holy Spirit and asking him: 'When I do this thing, what is it that drives my thought process? Where does this desire within me come from? What is its root?' Paul the apostle likes to talk about this in existential terms: 'Death is at work in us, but life is at work in you', but he leaves us encouraged: 'Do not lose heart. Though outwardly we are wasting away, yet inwardly we are being renewed day by day.'[21]

God is always making progress with us, even when we can't see it ourselves. Although spiritual transformation is no church picnic, we are not without the finest resources sent from heaven to help us.

WHY WOULD GOD TRUST US?

As a young Christian working for a busy London advertising agency, I won't deny that I found it tough working to a different rule book from others around me. There was a lot of excessive behaviour. It was challenging, taking a different path from others. On one occasion I failed spectacularly when the company won a major piece of new business. The company drink was freely flowing and being on a low salary . . . well, let's just say I took advantage of it and ended up making a bit of a fool of myself.

My boss said the next day, 'The trouble with you, Andrew, is that you have no strength of character.' It could have been the Holy Spirit speaking to me, maybe it was, but I realised in that instant, something needed to change – and it would take more than human willpower.

When our character fails us again and again it becomes just that bit harder to believe that God would ever want to use someone like us. And yet as Gandalf says, much to the chagrin of King Elrond, 'It is in men that we must place our hope.'[22]

It is why we continually need to welcome interruptions as gifts to break into our experiences and experiment more with our faith. How else, as Alan Coles suggests, will we produce a healthy 'harvest of life eternal'?[23]

We need to welcome interruptions brought by God and even pray for them daily to help us 'be alert' because we know the 'enemy the devil prowls around like a roaring lion looking for someone to devour'.[24]

WHEN A PATTEN OF BEHAVIOUR IS LEFT UNINTERRUPTED

Not all bad patterns of behaviour will land us in prison or see us do hours in the community. Some of it just covertly exists with us and has been going on for so long that it becomes the unspoken problem.

As Christians we can be incredibly law-abiding when it comes to rules, much like the Pharisees. Sorry, but when it comes to love we can be less certain of ourselves. As with Andrew Lloyd Webber's song, 'Love Changes Everything', it should change everything.

Besides, isn't this at the heart of our relationship with Jesus?

Over the years it is hard for failed change not to accumulate 'compound interest' in heartache and disappointment. We might even have forced ourselves to learn how to conceal it for the sake of keeping things moving, like my old VW Sharan.

A past lecturer of mine relayed a story of an older lady at her church who had come down the stairs one morning and sat at the kitchen table with her cup of tea, as she had done for many years, only to realise that she was no longer in love with her husband who was still asleep upstairs.

It was a wake-up moment.

She felt resentment, but it also scared her and made her feel guilty. The lady prayed and as she sat there the Holy Spirit brought to mind her wedding vows. She allowed them to invade her feelings and began to think that, if she had loved him once, why couldn't she love him again?

Over the coming months the elderly lady made it her daily discipline before God to actively love her husband. She chose to work with the habit, not the feeling. Slowly through a continual surrendering of her feelings a transformation began to happen.

Her first love for her husband returned. Her desire to love an imperfect man outweighed her desire to jack it in and walk away. Virgil, the Roman poet, may have said love conquers all, but it took the love of Jesus to provoke a selfless action to save a marriage.

When John, the disciple and apostle, declared that 'God is love'[25] it becomes a huge statement of intent. It is far from a Hallmark card with a saccharine sentiment. These small but huge words hold within them the ultimate hope to change the impossible and rescue the unreachable.

You in the Future

If we can stop to reflect where we have taken wrong turns with wrong choices in life, we will have taken a massive step forward to seeing the kingdom of God advance in our lives. We begin to move away from those thoughts and attitudes that have been allowed to darken our soul and deceived us into thinking real change is not possible.

Jesus is not just in us but Immanuel – with us.

And it has always been this way ever since we were born and he put his image in us. We have not always been spiritually awake to see it. So when you look at yourself in the mirror next, imagine Jesus in you and smiling back at you.

You are being changed by his glory, and his story is becoming your story, one day at a time. Be patient. It is happening. Here is a little spiritual exercise to help you move on and see more change.

INTERRUPTER

PRAYER EXERCISE: MEMORY PRAYER

A prayer to help you identify where something from the past may be distorting the perception you have of yourself.

1. Start by centring yourself on Jesus and remind yourself of his great love for you.

2. Ask the Holy Spirit to recall a time when you felt particularly close to Jesus. How did it affect you? Bathe awhile in this memory.

3. Ask the Holy Spirit to make you aware of any past words that may have shaped how you see yourself now. Maybe they have affected your confidence, even caused you to be hard on yourself. Speak to the Lord about it.

4. Remember, you are made in the image of God, not in the image of other people. Ask the Holy Spirit to break the power of those wrong thoughts and ask for his healing touch.

5. Finish by recalling some of your favourite words of Jesus. Let them shape your prayer so that you become aware of his mercy and abundant grace towards you.

'Yet this I call to mind and therefore I have hope.' (Lam. 3:21)

WHAT DIFFERENCE DOES IT MAKE?

There are many reasons why I love the Bible, but one of those is because I can see from beginning to end how it is one long account of individual lives being continually interrupted by God so he can reveal his love and purpose for their lives.

He began to draw my attention to himself while in lower school, when I was given a little red book. No, not the one with quotations by Chairman Mao Tse-Tung, but a small, bound version of the New Testament gifted by the Gideons.[3] At the front I found some helpful Bible verses to use when faced with trouble and difficult situations. And use them I did.

Later, I found out that God had an extended version out, which gave me another 39 books to read. It even included travel maps at the back just in case I found myself backpacking in the ancient Near East.

All the way through, from Abraham to Paul the apostle, I saw how ordinary lives were redirected by feuds, murder, slavery, imprisonment, wars, famine, illness and persecution. But it is how God lovingly interrupts them to bring a constant message of forgiveness, restoration and transformation that was to eventually make the Bible so appealing to me.

One of my all-time favourite stories of interruption is of the woman at the well in the town of Sychar in Samaria. At one level her story feels like one of those times when Jesus

> **THE WHOLE MAN IS TO DRINK JOY FROM THE FOUNTAIN OF JOY. AS AUGUSTINE SAID, THE RAPTURE OF THE SAVED SOUL WILL 'FLOW OVER' INTO THE GLORIFIED BODY."**
> C.S. LEWIS[1]

> **IN ALL THESE THINGS WE ARE MORE THAN CONQUERORS THROUGH HIM WHO LOVED US."**
> PAUL THE APOSTLE[2]

just happens to be around to help someone who needs help but, of course, that is never the case. God doesn't do 'random'.

The woman comes to the well at the hottest part of the day, when she knows no one else from the town will be around, but she soon discovers that she is not alone. Jesus asks for a drink, but her immediate response is to say that Jews don't associate with Samaritans.

Jesus goes on to tell her that if she knew who he was she would be the one asking him for a drink instead: 'Everyone who drinks this water will be thirsty again, but whoever drinks the water I give them will never thirst. Indeed, the water I give them will become in them a spring of water welling up to eternal life.'[4]

Jesus reveals the true state of her life by telling her that he knows about her five husbands and the man who is not her husband.

IDENTIFYING THE PATTERNS OF FAILURE

I have read this story many times over the years but what strikes me perhaps most about it is the obvious pattern of failure in each of her relationships. I have thought that each time she fails in a relationship she must take her pain and disappointment into the next one, hoping somehow the next time will be different from the last.

How easy it is to continue to make the wrong choices over and over again. We may promise ourselves we will be better next time and find a way to curb our bursts of anger, or our casual addiction to late-night scrolling of pornography, or our habit of drinking just a little bit too much too often because we have had another stressful day.

Like it or not, we are serial sinners, albeit ones being sanctified by grace, but it is frustrating all the same to repeat the same boring old sin. The solution is, of course, to break the cycle and for it to be replaced by something better than the problem. But it will have a better chance of happening if something interrupts us.

Statistics show that around 25 per cent of all prisoners released will become repeat offenders. The figure is even higher for those adults released after a custodial sentence of just 12 months, with a reoffending rate of 58.8 per cent.[5]

Prison Fellowship Ministries has a slogan, 'We believe no one is beyond hope. Do you?' In the UK they have created an army of

What Difference Does It Make? 141

3,000 volunteers to work across 120 prisons in England and Wales to make this hope a living reality. At its heart is mercy for the prisoner – whatever they have done.

Among the many things that we learn from Jesus' encounter with the woman at the well is how mercifully he deals with the habitual nature of sin. I like to think that when he met the woman he would have said under his breath, 'Sheesh! Enough is enough. Let's get you right!'

When I gave my life to Jesus I had more than a few unhealthy habits that needed to be broken in me. One of those was smoking. So on one wet and windy Sunday evening, feeling inspired by the vicar's talk, I came out of church with some friends, took my new packet of cigarettes and rather piously threw it into a nearby bin. I was cheered on by the others as we made our way to Burger King. But it took only five minutes for me to contemplate how rash I had been and so I secretly made my way back to the bin to retrieve the cigarettes. I was to learn a motivation to quit the next time would need a longer journey away from the next bin.

I was also, more importantly, to learn that it was not the habit of smoking or even the guilt of doing it that needed addressing, but the inward habits of the soul, out of which everything else could flow.

Of course, not all bad habits carry a health warning because we don't always see them as bad. They also tend to be ones we turn to when we need comfort. It became very apparent as a new Christian that I would need to learn some new habits if I had any chance of giving up some of my old habits.

St Augustine described a sacrament as an outward sign of an invisible grace, which he saw as a mysterious work that happens within but needs validation by an outward expression. It made me wonder if I could see everyday habits as forms of sacraments, as physical symbols of God being at work within me.

The beginning of change starts with the beginning of new habits, which in church language we like to call 'rituals', such as the regular breaking of bread, regular repentance, regular prayer, etc. It is these learnt habits within us that we also call 'spiritual disciplines' and which the Holy Spirit uses to transform and bring wholeness of life.

Our contentment within will always want to challenge the discontent of our exterior lifestyle. It will always want to change something to bring us into closer communion with the Father. But more often than not it will need an interruption.

142   *Life, Interrupted*

The Samaritan woman's daily ritual was to come to collect water when no one else was around. It was as much a pattern of her life as her serial relationships. Unless something breaks the pattern, it is simply 'business as usual'.

This is what guilt and shame will do. It will want you to continue to hide away from nice respectable people and find a way to carry on.

LIVING IN CRAZYVILLE

Putting aside human relationships, we can be equally challenged with our relationships with money, position or power. But I don't always see many guilty faces around. Flaunting wealth and position are nothing new, of course, because human insecurity is nothing new. The external life wants to dictate to the interior life which way to go and, left unattended, it can easily throw a cloak over the 'lamp on the stand' and cause us to stumble in the darkness.

Mark Lutz says how easy it is to reside in a place he calls, 'Crazyville . . . a state where all truth becomes our personal truth'.[6] You can see the logic here. Although the people there may not see it, their rules on how to behave and act are different from ours. He calls the other place, where 'normal ones' live, 'Homeland'. This is where we live with the rules that, for example, if we do something wrong and hurt somebody, we will be open to correction, not least when we have been an idiot.

What is more, we know the best thing for our relationship is to ask for forgiveness. That is normal behaviour. Back in Crazyville, no wrongdoing can be admitted because there is no real understanding that anything is wrong with our behaviour, so why feel guilty about it?

Unless everyone lives in the same land, using the same rules as us, there will always be tension. We will then do what we all do when conflicted. We either get angry, cry victim when challenged or hide ourselves away maybe in a task or a hobby or another relationship. In fact, anywhere where we can avoid our version of truth being challenged by another truth.

We may ask: How do you get someone to leave Crazyville and join you in the Homeland? The answer Lutz says is to present a new model of normal, by sharing a vision of another possible option. Because up to this point, someone may have never been shown another way to live. You might be the 'streetlamp' God wants to use to help guide them home.

What Difference Does It Make?   143

THINGS THAT YOU CAN'T JUST GET OVER

Any psychiatrist will tell you that shame is a key factor in the cycle of abuse. It is the one thing that will stop you from getting help. And you do need external help because shame is not something you just get over.

The worst part of all this is that you will continue to suffer, and the pain will just multiply as it finds a way to get passed on, with you becoming either the abuser or the continually abused. I know this all sounds rather depressing, but sadly the studies show this to be true. And if you are female and want further proof, over 50 per cent of women in our prisons are victims of domestic abuse before they go on to be a criminal.[7]

No wonder Jesus showed mercy to the precious woman in Samaria. Without him showing up and interrupting her day, the cycle of abuse would have continued. And how many more lives would have been wrecked apart from her own?

Some years ago, working as a consultant, I sat in a meeting with people from an advertising agency. Afterwards, I found myself alone with Ian (not his real name), the owner of the company. He knew I was a Christian and said to me rather unexpectedly,

'I wish I could have your faith.'

I replied, 'You can.'

'Nah!' he said. 'I did something stupid when I was younger while off backpacking in Australia and I can't forgive myself.'

At that moment I felt my heart pulse as the Holy Spirit gave me a 'word of knowledge' (a piece of personal information about a person supernaturally given by the Holy Spirit). 'Did you get a girl pregnant and force her to have an abortion?'

Ian's eyes instantly welled up. 'Yes!'

He told me that he had been constantly living with the shame of putting pressure on this girl to get rid of her baby so as not to damage his career. Ian could not think why on earth God would want to forgive someone like him – largely because he had no way to forgive himself.

I remember that I spoke of the cross and how it was big enough for all our guilt and shame, allowing for every conceivable sin to be forgiven. That day in that conference room, Ian showed amazing faith and courage and prayed a prayer of repentance and accepted Jesus into his life. I saw a broken man who had no way of forgiving himself restored and healed. I swear he walked out of that room two inches taller than when he first walked in.

I suspect the woman at the well was just trying to conceal her pain and get through life the best way she could, much like my friend Ian. She knew she was far from perfect. She was undoubtedly a long way from the life she had dreamed for herself as a young girl.

At times we can believe we don't deserve any better. And that is even for those of us who have a relationship with Jesus. We feel we have had our chance and blown it through a dumb decision or wrong action. It can mean we now choose to live a quieter life 'under the radar'. But have you noticed how easily we condemn ourselves and forget exactly the vast height and extreme width of the cross?

How easily we can believe the lie that we are the worst person on earth, and nothing can save us from ourselves. We can even make a habit of believing that, so much so that we lose all confidence. But it is here that John the apostle gives hope: 'If our hearts do not condemn us, we have confidence before God and receive from him anything we ask, because we keep his commands and do what pleases him.'[8]

It seems to me that the well in Samaria is a metaphor for all that was habitually wrong in the woman's life. The empty water pot could easily symbolise the need for her life to be filled with something better than what the world could give her. The woman is not just carrying an empty water pot, but the weight of the world on her shoulders. It becomes an outward expression of all that is missing in her life. It is the visible sign of the invisible pain in her cycle of sin.

Habitual sin is just another phrase for addiction; if not broken, it is something that enslaves our thinking, time and energy, and often steals our joy.

KILLING THE SPIDER

Carlos Whittaker describes the problem of habitual sin as being like a spider. When we walk into a spider's web and try to knock it away, it will always find a way to come back again unless we deal with it properly. Unless we 'kill the spider', the source of the problem, we will always remain a victim in its web.

What Difference Does It Make?   145

Whitaker says, 'The spider is the agreement you make with a lie and the web is the self-medicating behaviour that brings false comfort to the lie.'[9] For some that self-medication might be extreme retail shopping. For others, it might be pornography, gluttony or even serial affairs.

Perhaps it is possible to see the woman's coming to the well at the most physically punishing time of the day was not just as the daily reminder of her chosen life, but also of how it had become scarred with the self-medicated need for continued affairs.

Whatever our back story, it is always a good day when Jesus turns up. She would come to see the interruption break her pattern of habitual sin through a revelatory 'How did I get here?' moment. Jesus breaks the cycle, restores the woman and resets her life – all over lunch.

In my experience, when Jesus breaks into our lives to challenge sin it is never without an invitation to be forgiven. It also comes with a restoration plan to break old patterns of behaviour to renew life, which means putting himself at the centre of it. As Richard Rohr remarks, 'God's forgiveness is like breathing. Forgiveness is not apparently something God does; it is who God is. God can do no other.'[10]

Unlike taking the wrong direction on the motorway and feeling we have gone too far to turn back, we can discover the opposite, make the U-turn and rediscover joy.

There is always a way back.

Love always beats the odds.

It resets the past with renewed hope.

It is merciful, loving and kind.

Because God is merciful, loving and kind.

Love will always be enough.

It sets you free and forgives.

It gives back your future and dreams.

In him you will find your joy.

WAKEFULNESS

In his apocalyptic writing, John the apostle speaks to the church at Sardis, a fellowship that is apparently running on autopilot.

Sardis itself was the ancient capital that was well known for having once been a great city. In the first century, at the time of John's writing, it had become a symbol of commercial success. Its past wealth and power should have helped make it impregnable, but complacency had meant it had fallen twice in the past – both through night attacks.

The church, like the city, had now got a reputation for being a mirror image of this once great place. It reflected the city's cultural values and not the values of the 'City of God', to quote St Augustine. And like this once great ancient place, it had switched off 'at the wheel' and allowed its over-confidence to make itself vulnerable to worldly thinking.

It is not that it hadn't been busy trying to do the stuff, but for all its efforts it hadn't produced the right kind of fruit – the fruit of the Spirit. As Jesus said in his memorable sermon, 'No good tree bears bad fruit, nor does a bad tree bear good fruit. Each tree is recognised by its own fruit.'[11] The church had drifted and, like a driver at the wheel, unless given a nudge it would not end well for them.

How often we think we are doing okay. We believe we have got a handle on what is right and wrong, but secretly we may not be quite so sure if our values are God's or the world's. However, because we have given our life to it, we still believe it may be enough to bring us through. What is more, we think it is all right with God. I mean, it is not that we are bad people, right?

UPWARDS AND ONWARDS

Here's a small confession.

I have always wanted to run up an escalator the wrong way.

It was at a local department store. I had made sure that no one was on it, as if to show at least some partial responsibility, and then as quickly as I could I ran all the way up the moving stairs. If you want to get to the top, you can't stand still for one moment because if you do, you will find yourself right at the bottom again.

It took longer than I had thought, but it was incredibly satisfying to have made it to the top. Okay, I know it is not quite Ben Nevis. There might even be some CCTV footage somewhere. Who knows? But putting aside my confession to you, it feels like a picture of the spiritual battle we are in.

What Difference Does It Make?   147

There is a need for us to stay disciplined in keeping moving towards the kingdom of heaven – even when we feel life is against us. We can't for one moment switch off and think things will be where we leave them. Sadly, they won't – so don't fall for the illusion. And if you don't believe me, can I recommend the escalator at the Bentall's Centre in Kingston-upon-Thames? Joking, please don't!

This is why we get so frustrated when we come before God in prayer and don't feel we have made any progress.

As I have said, our habits will either make or break us, but they also have the potential to define us and our relationship with God and one another. It really is as simple as that.

You and I know it is easy to tick the boxes with our daily devotional times. If you are anything like me, you know you can read a passage of Scripture, pray a prayer, and then a little later completely forget what you have just read and prayed.

Not wanting to put you too much on the spot (or maybe I am), if you were to do an audit of your devotional week, you might find some encouragement in being able to plot how many times you read your Bible, worshipped or how many minutes you spent alone with God.

There is now even an app that counts the minutes you pray to help you beat your personal best, but might I suggest you don't make a virtue out of your devotional time! In the words of Nike, 'Just do it.'

For myself, I wake up most mornings, go to the armchair in the snug room and become still. Gratitude is always my first and last prayer. I will centre myself on Jesus, seek his presence. At times my thoughts will stray, but I take him with me in them. After all, it could be the Holy Spirit taking me there.

I will meditate on Scripture. Not always very much. Maybe I will read some reflective writing and, even though there are things to do and places to go, I know I have begun the making of a habit, a ritual, a pattern for my spiritual life.

My devotional time has become an intentional interruption to the start of my day. In truth, it takes some effort, much like running up an escalator the wrong way. I also fail, constantly, and find myself back at the bottom, but once you have seen the view from the top it is always worth going again.

The risks of being changed by these planned daily interruptions are high, but so are the stakes. Jesus says to the church at Sardis: 'Wake up! Strengthen what remains and is about to die, for I have found your deeds unfinished in the sight of my God. Remember, therefore, what you have received and heard; hold it fast, and repent. But if you do not wake up, I will come like a thief, and you will not know at what time I will come to you.'[12]

John Sweet comments that the message to Sardis is 'a wake-up call to stay alert in the darkest times and to be reminded that life is filled with vast opportunities and dangers.'[13] I find it hard not to think of Jesus' words to his disciples in the garden of Gethsemane: 'Watch and pray so that you will not fall into temptation. The spirit is willing, but the flesh is weak.'[14]

There is a Greek word which preachers love to pull off their shelves when talking about repentance: *metanoia.* But its meaning goes much deeper than just about confessing sin. Tertullian said it was about a change of mind. The word used in Latin is maybe more recognisable to us: *conversiōn-em*, which we translate as 'to turn around.'

This is the experience of the woman at the well in Samaria. After she accepts Jesus' invitation to drink from the well of living water she *turns around* and goes back to the town to tell others about a man who told her everything she had ever done. Her action symbolises her repentance and readiness to move on with her restored life.

As with the neural experience of a Default Mode Network, there will be times when we find ourselves switching off, so it is comforting for us to know that God is still at work in us, but I have found it is invariably the interruption that startles me into saying, 'How on earth did I get here?' But when God interrupts it always comes with an opportunity to turn around and reset life.

THE INTERRUPTION AT THE WELL

At the time of the East Anglian revival of 1921, Revd Douglas Brown gave a wonderful sermon called 'The Left Water Pot.'[15] It is based on the story of the woman at the well; he imagines all the reasons why she might have left her water jar behind.

It is worth thinking about the significance of that clay vessel.

What Difference Does It Make?   149

Did she simply forget it? I mean, there was a lot of new information being taken in.

Did she simply leave it behind so she could run quicker to tell others of the good news?

Or maybe there was another reason.

Jesus had asked her for a drink of water, but he had come to the well with nothing to hold it in. She was now a sin-free woman. The cycle of abuse had been broken. Years of guilt and shame had been lifted. Where maybe words failed her, perhaps she could show her gratitude by leaving the jar for Jesus to use.

Maybe it was the only way at hand that she could use to begin to show gratitude for all that Jesus had just done for her. I guess you and I will never know until we meet this woman one day for ourselves, but this we can know:

- Love always wants to find us.
- Love always wants to heal us.
- Love always wants to cancel the debt of sin.

It is Jesus' first and last thought to put himself between us and the thing that causes us to stumble and fall.

This is what makes the rough, splintery cross that held Jesus outside Jerusalem's walls so powerful. The highly effective Roman method of human torture, designed to cause maximum pain and strike psychological fear into the minds of oppressed peoples, has its power usurped by a greater power and becomes the ultimate symbol of love.

Death is replaced with life. It is the ultimate symbol of the disruption of sin.

Its presence holds a shadow that is big enough to fall on any of us. It has the power to heal and restore us from any habitual sin and the causes of continual shame.

With our own encounter with Jesus, we are invited to leave our own 'water pots' behind. I can even see a picture of the cross with millions of discarded water pots all around it, all shapes and sizes, all of them symbols of burdens being lifted and of lives being turned around. It is a glorious scene!

I want to give another reason why the woman may have left her water pot behind.

Have you ever considered that maybe she had already planned to come back? The woman had tasted life-giving water and wanted it, not for a day, but for a lifetime. An interruption to a broken life that is restored will do this to you.

Through his interruptions Jesus will open the way for the Holy Spirit to overflow into all our lives: our relationships, past disappointments, bad decisions – even into our worst character traits.

Jesus is unstoppable . . . unconditionally merciful . . . unendingly loving . . . impossibly kind . . . extravagantly generous . . . full stop.

THE BUCKET PRAYER
(BASED ON JOHN 4:1-29)

Lord Jesus, I come with my empty bucket to your well.

I arrive feeling ashamed and wanting to hide my sin from you.

You know how I fill my life with worthless things.

Deep down I know that my every need is met only in you.

Thank you for interrupting my life with your love for me.

Although I never find correction easy,

I choose to turn away from my sin and repent, asking for forgiveness.

Replenish me, renew my mind, and give rest for my soul.

Slake my thirst and fill me with your living, giving water.

Send me out empty of my burdens and full of hope.

For yours is the kingdom. To God be the glory. Amen.

12 INTERCESSION AS INTERRUPTION

I was invited by my French CEO to attend with him and to speak at a marketing directors' breakfast meeting in Paris. I was flattered to be asked and quickly said 'yes', not least because it was in Paris.

He asked, 'How's your French?'

'Pardon moi?'

You might already be ahead of me here.

Over the years I had been on a number of family holidays in mid-west France, so I thought I might have grasped just enough French to get me by. Such was my confidence over the next month that I prepared my speech, created my presentation slides and practised the content with the CEO. I was all set.

We arrived by Eurostar at Gare du Nord and made our way to a central hotel. The conference room was set out for fifty or so people, which felt more than a little intimidating to this Brit. The breakfast buffet had that wonderful aroma you might expect from a French patisserie. There were silver plates of warm *croissants aux amandes* and *pain au chocolat* waiting, along with tall glasses of *jus d'orange pressé*. Pots of freshly brewed coffee were sitting next to an army of small white cups laid out in perfect symmetry. As I said, all rather intimidating.

"ALL SHALL BE AMEN AND ALLELUIA."
ST AUGUSTINE OF HIPPO[1]

"BECAUSE JESUS LIVES FOREVER, HE HAS A PERMANENT PRIESTHOOD. THEREFORE HE IS ABLE TO SAVE COMPLETELY THOSE WHO COME TO GOD THROUGH HIM, BECAUSE HE ALWAYS LIVES TO INTERCEDE FOR THEM."
HEBREWS 7:24-5

I was eventually introduced and invited up on stage, and I launched off into my best French. As I began, a hand went up on the middle row. I chose to ignore it and gestured that I would like to continue, but a few minutes later another hand went up. This one was more persistent. Having tried the avoidance strategy, I moved into the denial stage, but this person was clearly not giving up. Eventually, I was forced to stop. I took a breath and said, '*Oui?*'

I kid you not, I did not understand a single word that was said next. I even asked the person to repeat it, only for their words to sound less intelligible than the first time round.

I froze.

I had not considered that Parisians speak fast and in 'business French'. As it happens, it is quite a different French from mine. The interruption turned into a disruption. Not only could I not answer the question, but I was completely thrown and left unable to speak any kind of coherent French. Although I still maintained enough to be able to ask for the bill.

Trying to continue as normal through an interruption is tough. At some point we will need to accept that the interruption has become a disruption. But we know that while it is still an interruption there is a possibility to return to what came before. A disruption won't afford us that dignity.

We may even try to control the disruption with a passive reasoning with it and ourselves. In fact, anything to try not to lose control. It also has the power to bring some kind of conflict and chaos to our emotional and spiritual wellbeing, which makes it a lot harder to dismiss – much like an interrupting French businessperson.

THE SUFFERING OF THE SOUL IS REAL

It is in the uncertain times that we must find a way to trust the Disrupter, the one who entered the darkness and brought light into the world.

You will remember in the summer of 2014 the Islamic State of Iraq and Syria (known better as ISIS) attacked and occupied a large area in Iraq. Caught in the middle of this war were the ancient Christian churches of that area.

Christians were seen as a western enemy and many of them were forced to flee from their family homes and businesses under the spray of bullets. Those who stayed, often the ones without the financial or physical means to escape, along with courageous priests, did their best to survive with the help of ministries such as Open Doors.

In the autumn of 2016, ISIS was overthrown, but returning Christians found many of their houses and churches robbed, emptied and destroyed.

Christians in Iraq remain uneasy. The future is far from certain. But get this: in the last hundred years there hasn't been a single decade of peace. Not one. Many Iraqis suffer from trauma-related symptoms. Depression and mental illness are big problems.

Brother Wisam, a monk who lives outside the Christian city of Qaraqosh, said, 'If we don't deal with the trauma in our community, the future of Christianity in Iraq is very dark.'[2]

Persecuted Christians struggle to get rid of the anger inside of them, which has the further effect of triggering conflict in their families. People suffer from sleeplessness, and thoughts of suicide are not uncommon among young people.[3]

It is hard for Iraqi Christians to keep trusting in God when neighbours who they have known for many years suddenly turn on them, breathing murderous threats and looting their homes. Life will never be as it was before. And this is what some disruptions do. They move you to an experience of discomfort, disillusionment and pain.

How difficult it is to see these times as something that any good could emerge from.

Whether it is war, persecution, chronic condition or terminal illness, it is hard to believe how life can ever be more than it was before. It makes it that much harder to trust God when we can't control the outcome, but it appears that we can't have one without the other, as C.S. Lewis says: 'Try to exclude the possibility of suffering which the order of nature and the existence of free wills involve, and you find that you have excluded life itself.'[4]

All the while, as the psychologist Carl Jung says, we battle with our 'shadow self', which is the unconscious part of our character that does not line up with how we would like to see ourselves. It means when we see imperfection, we will want to resist, reject or suppress that side of us. It can leave us disliking ourselves for failing not to be better than we think we are. Worst still, we project those feelings of dislike onto others to make us feel better about our own faults. Jung had a name for this too – ego ideal.

We all wish our imperfect sides, our character flaws could be battered away with a bit of prayer at church, but our God of love doesn't seem to see things as we do!

The point of prayer is not to provide us with an instant hit of happiness, but to lead our hearts and minds into a more profound experience of him – which must involve a cross and an empty tomb in equal measure. It means we must find a way to live in faith with the mystery that God is always doing more behind our backs than he shows to our face.

This doesn't have to be seen as a cop-out, but a sanity-saver. Unlike C.S. Lewis, I cannot offer a pithy one-liner on why such terrible suffering was allowed to happen to Iraqi Christians, but what I do know is that there are now growing churches in Iraq and Syria made up entirely of new believers from other faiths because ordinary and brave Christians continued to believe and find a way to love God and love their neighbour as themselves.

JESUS THE DISRUPTER

Jesus is walking along the road with his disciples when they come across a man begging, who has been blind from birth. The disciples, curious to know why he was born suffering, ask: 'Rabbi, who sinned, this man or his parents, that he was born blind?'[5]

This is a big 'lean in' moment.

All ears are now tuned in to hear what Jesus is going to say, but on first impressions it looks as though he blows the opportunity. He chooses to give no medical reason. There is no family history trauma discussed or any mention of a tragic accident. No generational sin or episode is brought out of the closet. Jesus simply says, 'This has happened so that the works of God might be displayed in him.'[6]

He then picks up some dirt from the ground, mixes it with his own saliva, puts it on the blind man's eyes and tells him to go and wash it off in the pool of Siloam.

Some biblical scholars think this might be a reference to the creation story in Genesis and is used by Jesus to remind us that before all else we all come from dust and are made in his glory. Whatever is intended, we see a man's sight wonderfully restored and saved from living rough on the streets.

I suspect, just as it is today, suffering remained a complex question – or maybe simply it was a distraction from something else going on here. Either way, Jesus comes as the Disrupter just as God disrupts the darkness in Genesis to speak light. 'I am the light of the world,' says Jesus.[7]

The Son of God comes as the Disrupter to challenge the status quo, and points to the human failures and difficulties of upholding moral and legal practices of an ancient law without true faith and a relationship with God. Jesus shows how the Pharisees suffer from spiritual blindness while the people live in a darkness and need the gift of light.

It takes a step of faith but if we can see there is a bigger plan to see his glory revealed it will bring us comfort. St Augustine says, 'Let us understand that God is a physician, and that suffering is medicine for salvation, not a punishment for damnation.'[8]

MIRACLES AS DISRUPTIONS

Michael[9] was someone whose life had been derailed by a long-term medical condition and came to us out of desperation – thankfully.

One Tuesday lunch-time he walked into our church office. In fact, right up to our desks and requested Emma and me to pray for him there and then. Before us stood a big-framed man who had all the looks of someone who was a ghost of their former self. One of our volunteers at Storehouse, our compassion programme, had told Michael that our church believed in healing prayer and so he had come to seek us out.

We listened intently to how he had lived in misery with colitis for the last twenty-six years, which had severely damaged his intestines and forced him to wear a colostomy bag, which brought with it deep shame. Over the years, there had been three life-saving operations and around one hundred and fifty emergency hospital admissions. In two days' time, he was due to have a procedure that would be irreversible and see him wearing a catheter for the rest of his life.

Emma and I didn't ask to know any more than he had told us. He just wanted us to pray, so we simply did what we have done on so many other occasions: we invited the Holy Spirit to come and minister in power.

We held out our hands and prayed for God's love to be poured out over him. We prayed for no more than a couple of minutes before Michael looked up and said he felt warmth through his whole body. We told him it was Jesus showing his love for him. And within five minutes he was gone.

Two days later, on the Thursday afternoon, Michael phoned and sounded different.

He told me that the consultant was baffled at the final X-ray. It showed his bladder as being totally pink, like new. All black lesions had gone. There were no signs of damage or inflammation at all. The consultant held up the last X-ray with an earlier one to see the difference. He even got a second opinion and ran further tests just to make sure his eyes weren't deceiving him.

This wonderful man was completely healed. What's more, it was medically verified.

When we had a chance later to meet up, I asked what Michael was now looking forward to the most, and he rather excitedly said, 'Swimming!' He hadn't been in the water for twenty-six years.

He attended an Alpha group and became a Christian. His testimony was so powerful that an atheist and one other person became Christians and eventually got baptised with him. He had spent so many years disliking himself and hating his situation that his transformation was truly remarkable.

GOD LOVES TO DISRUPT DARKNESS WITH LIGHT

But of course, not everyone is miraculously healed. When I was in my twenties, an enthusiastic and well-meaning pastor was convinced my blind right eye was going to be healed but, after many times of prayer and asking, I still wait. Although the injury disrupted my life, cost me a job and meant I had to give up playing cricket, I am not depressed. And here's why.

I have been blessed by God in more ways than I could ever imagine. The light has outshone the darkness, so much so the injury has become an irrelevance. God's love will continue to work through every interruption and disruption – and nothing can stop it. Because that's what love does.

LIVING IN A WORLD OF INTENTIONAL DISRUPTERS

In the business world, much is written about 'disrupter brands'. These are brands that are game changers that challenge traditional models of practice. Think Uber or Amazon and you get the point.

They are outsiders, rule-breakers, mischief-makers.

They infuriate and irritate traditionalists.

They are the courageous ones who refuse to be silenced.

They see what others don't.

As there was a blindness in the Pharisees who couldn't see a relationship with God outside a set of rules, so it is with those bent on defending the status quo. You will sometimes hear them called 'dinosaurs' and we all know what happened to them!

Back in 1997 just 101 words were uttered in a ground-breaking TV commercial on a backdrop of famous names that would herald a digital revolution.

> Here's to the crazy ones. The misfits. The rebels. The troublemakers. The round pegs in the square holes. The ones who see things differently. They're not fond of rules. And they have no respect for the status quo. You can quote them, disagree with them, glorify or vilify them. About the only thing you can't do is ignore them. Because they change things. They push the human race forward. And while some may see them as the crazy ones, we see genius. Because the people who are crazy enough to think they can change the world, are the ones who do.[10]

Apple made history with its 'Think Different' brand strategy, which reversed its market share decline to make it one of the world's largest companies. These words lit the blue touch paper and became a clarion call to a new generation of business entrepreneurs. It tore up the rule book without asking anyone permission. It was quite audacious, exciting and just a little bit scary.

Jesus is no Steve Jobs. He is so much more. He is the Son of the Most High God, the Messiah, Saviour of the world, the King of kings, queens, princes, princesses and paupers.

He is also another thing – offensive. Jesus loves to offend the mind to expose the heart.

He is Aslan, the lion with a terrifying roar but with the purr of endless compassion.

INTERCESSORS AS INTERRUPTERS

I am sure it is not just me, but we can all be tempted to see some of our prayers as having a limited effect to change circumstances. So much so – even though we won't dare say it out loud – we don't think it will make a jot of difference and things will happen regardless. And that secretly scares us. It is perhaps also the area of prayer that makes us feel most guilty. John Ortberg quotes his mentor, Dallas Willard, to make the point: 'The idea that everything would happen exactly as it does regardless of whether we pray or not is a spectre that haunts the minds of many who sincerely profess belief in God. It makes prayer psychologically impossible, replacing it with dead ritual at best.'[11]

We are tempted to use an approach for healing prayer with a caveat such as 'if it is your will' or we bottle out completely and simply ask 'for peace and comfort' for the person. Dialling down our prayers says more about dialling down our expectations than believing God can do the impossible.

We like to give ourselves a fall-back position. It is what makes those requests by vagabonds and victims, the lame and the shamed in the gospels such compelling reading. These are the kind of people Jesus loves to welcome – the ones who believe in him for the impossible, the ones who have nothing and give everything.

Jesus had nothing but compassion for the lost and broken, with a spiritual authority way above the Pharisees' and scribes' pay scale. If you are not seeing more healings and breakthroughs, maybe ask yourself: Are you praying audacious prayers or safe prayers? Whose reputation are you really defending?

While I have been saying in this book that interruptions are invitations to change, there are also times when we interrupt heaven.

SEEING INTERCESSION AS INTERRUPTION

Intercession is where we ask for God's favour on behalf of someone else. And it is something we are encouraged to do rather than just sit back and say, 'Well, that's just the way things are and how they are going to be.'

John's Gospel records how Jesus intercedes for his disciples, knowing that they are going to need all of heaven's resources for what comes next.

Intercession as Interruption 161

> Holy Father, protect them by the power of your name, the name you gave me, so that they may be one as we are one. While I was with them, I protected them and kept them safe by that name you gave me. None has been lost except the one doomed to destruction so that Scripture would be fulfilled. I am coming to you now, but I say these things while I am still in the world, so that they may have the full measure of my joy within them.[12]

Intercession is persistent and won't take 'no' for an answer. Jesus encourages his disciples to be persistent in prayer, as in the parable of the persistent widow who kept coming to the judge with her demands for justice until in the end he was fed up to the back teeth with her and granted her request. In the same way we should pray and not give up easily.

Intercession stands up in a courtroom and refuses to be silenced by the prosecution and the judge's gavel. It is the place where we put ourselves between the situation and God, and appeal to his loving, all-compassionate nature.

And because we are moved to care our language is often affected by raw emotion. It is at times impertinent, rude, shameless, without poetic nuance or pauses. It is undignified, unrefined and feels more like haggling with a market trader than the polite language of prayer used in Sunday services.

You see, when we intercede, we are inviting the kingdom of God to break in and fix the injustices in his world, to break the chains of human suffering and give hope to the poor, to set the captives free and restore the sight of the blind.

We invite the kingdom of heaven to break into Satan's kingdom to bust his chops and see what has been stolen by sin given back. As Paul reassures us: 'Who then is the one who condemns? No one. Christ Jesus who died – more than that, who was raised to life – is at the right hand of God and is also interceding for us.'[13]

Jesus' ministry on earth may have lasted just three years but he has been interceding for us ever since. In fact, non-stop for the last two thousand years and he continues to speak to the Father on our behalf today – even as you read these words.

INTERRUPTER

DISRUPTER PRAYER

Jesus is a disrupter. It is through him that we will see the greatest changes and where we will acquire our strength and steel to stay on the narrow path. Prayer disrupts the enemy's plans. It allows God's kingdom to enter in to bring conviction and greater connection, and for his will to be done. Through himself he gives us access to heaven's richest assets.

So what do you want to see Jesus disrupt in your life today? Do you need a miracle or an intervention?

Make a note of three things that instantly come to your mind and say this disrupter prayer or be free to use a prayer of your own.

Lord Jesus, through your holy and powerful name.
I ask you to disrupt those things that have got a hold of me.
Where storms rage around me, bring your calm.
Where the ground sinks beneath me, be my rock.
Where my mood gets darkened, be my light.
Where my mind is worried, be my peace.
For you are my salvation, my strength,
my stronghold and deliverer.
Come, Holy Spirit. Come in grace.
Amen.

🔲 STIR IT UP!

Near to where I used to live there is an ancient Augustinian priory that dates to 1538 and is home to a community of some amazing friars. It is situated in the beautiful Stour Valley in south Suffolk and has John Constable's river running past its back door. Not a bad place to do community. Nearby are the ruined remains of a motte and bailey castle, which was later improved by stone, and was home to Elizabeth de Clare in the fourteenth century.

Today it is just a ghost of days gone past. From the top of the motte you can look down and see where the moat water stops, where the land has been filled in over the years. The sheltered water is covered by a green blanket of algae and lies completely undisturbed. Although beautiful at a distance underneath the surface lies quite a different story.

Left unstirred by a constant lack of movement, the water has become stagnant. While the river nearby brims with life, accompanied by anglers armed with their rods and vacuum flasks, the only thing you will catch here is a mouthful of mosquitos and gnats.

Stagnant water is unpleasant stuff. It gets cloudy, discoloured and after a time it smells rank. It is the perfect breeding ground for bacteria, bugs and parasites, so when I look down from the castle, I am not just looking at a bucolic scene but 'dead water'.

However, just one thing would change everything and bring it back to life.

> **"**
>
> **THOU HAST TAUGHT ME, SILENT RIVER! MANY A LESSON, DEEP AND LONG; THOU HAST BEEN A GENEROUS GIVER; I CAN GIVE THEE BUT A SONG."**
> HENRY WADSWORTH LONGFELLOW[1]

> **"**
>
> **KNOW THE TRUTH, AND THE TRUTH WILL SET YOU FREE."**
> JOHN 8:32

OXYGEN

Dissolved oxygen, as it is called, is essential for water. It enables fish and other aquatic organisms to live. When air is mixed with water it removes the poisonous and harmful carbon dioxide which, left alone, will cause high acidity.

Oxygen is something we all share. We all need air in our lungs or gills, if we are to stay healthy and alive. And here in the moat this can happen only when there is an interaction between air and water.

Apart from aquatic plants, which can draw on the sunlight (photosynthesis), one of the best ways to re-oxygenate water is to disturb the surface. This is what makes the wind such a powerful force. It can break into the surface of water to push the air underneath and oxygenate it by stirring it up.

Equally powerful is the inflow of water from a stream or river. Moving water is oxygen-rich and helps to replenish the old water by creating underwater turbulence. Through both the elements of wind and flowing waters they can do what the stagnant mosquito-infested water can't do for itself – bring it back to life and make it healthy again.

But without the constant interruption of flowing water or a moving wind nothing can happen. Also, one interruption is not enough, it needs the continued presence of a change agent to keep standing water healthy. To be left alone is the worst thing that can happen to it.

MOVEMENT

Movement gives meaning, and it is no wonder that God uses a nomadic free people in the wilderness to make the point. A people on the move allows him to begin a new movement, built on a two-way relationship with himself by instructing the hearts to know how to live, become resilient and to be able to face the future with confidence.

There are meant to be times when we need to learn to stop, look around and ask the question: Is my faith flowing with life or becoming stagnant?

I am not sure many people set out to live an untruthful life either to themselves or others, but how easily truth gets distorted when we are closed to being challenged.

This is the danger of sheltered thinking. It isolates and keeps us in a place of ignorance, robbing us of the experience to ebb and flow with every big or small interruption. Only when we are in open waters, where we allow ourselves to be in places of risk, will we progress as pilgrims. Otherwise, we will be trapped in closed waters, those places in our minds where we are stubborn to entertain any change for fear of losing control of who we are. But it will only see us rebreathing our own fetid air of delusion that we had any real control in the first place.

To isolate ourselves from external views does not keep us pure but creates an echo chamber for our thoughts. It can even end up being suffocating and stifle the soul. So maybe it is helpful to wonder, if not shudder, how different things would be if God did not allow constant interruptions – good or bad.

WHAT IF TRUTH LEFT US ALONE?

What if we were left alone to make all our decisions, control every outcome and were unstoppable?

What if every choice was based purely on our own version of wisdom and virtue?

I am not so sure it would end that well or, for that matter, leave us where we want to be. Simply putting 'cotton wool' around us to stop external forces interrupting us is not realistic or, more to the point, even an option, thankfully.

If we can see that not all interruptions hinder the quality of life, but could enhance it, they could be the gifts we need to keep our soul well. Peter the apostle says: 'When life gets really difficult, don't jump to the conclusion that God isn't on the job. Instead, be glad that you are in the very thick of what Christ experienced. This is a spiritual refining process, with glory just around the corner.'[2]

Interruptions are normal. In fact, worry if they are not there!

At the start of this book, I spoke about how I contracted Covid-19 in May 2020, which then turned into Long Covid for twenty months. I had a heavy uncomfortable pressure in my chest caused by inflammation around my lungs, which made it hard to breathe and talk for very long. I couldn't walk far without becoming exhausted. Walking around the garden was enough. At night it was just as uncomfortable in bed.

Worse still, my brain was like mush, which made it hard for me to concentrate on anything for too long. It was frustrating not to be able to absorb anything meaningfully that I read.

The simplest prayers became difficult. Trying to see God was like peering through a dense fog. My daily routines, liturgies for life, regular acts of worship, had come to a grinding halt. It was as if my life had stopped moving, much like a river that had stopped flowing – and at one point I feared my days were becoming increasingly stagnant in meaning.

On one occasion I remember sitting in a chair being still, not so much being prayerful, but stewing and quietly complaining to God for allowing this to happen to me when I had so much to do.

Quite honestly, at times, I was quite miffed with God. I resented not having the strength to see my family or be well enough to talk on Zoom. I was equally irritated by the fact that I could not lead the church well. While I saw on social media and WhatsApp groups how other leaders were stepping up, I felt I was doing nothing of value. It was as if my purpose was being taken away from me. It even began to make me feel like an abject failure.

It was a dark time.

DISTORTED JUDGEMENT

When life becomes cloudy and unclear, have you noticed how it affects our judgement? Something big might disrupt our lives and slow us down, like a chronic illness, job loss or a breakdown of a relationship, but unless we find a way to move on, we will begin to stagnate.

Socrates said to move the world we must first move ourselves, but when you feel left unmotivated by a difficult experience any kind of movement becomes a challenge. If we can't see a way forward, we can become incapacitated and, when we do, we should not be too surprised when our world-view becomes discoloured. To others, on the surface everything might look normal, even peaceful, but underneath there is that sense within us of an abnormality about the situation.

I had to have the uncomfortable conversation with God about what would happen if I never got well. Remember, at the time we still knew very little about Covid-19. I had to find a way to come to terms with

Stir It Up! 167

whatever was before me and trust him that he had control of my situation.

But when you are in stagnant waters, it can easily make you apathetic and distort your judgement.

King David should have been at war with his army, but his poor decision led him into adultery, which would result in a contrived plan to save face by killing the wronged husband. God interrupted David's sordid affair with Bathsheba by sending a prophet to speak some home truths.[3] The revelation was devastating for the young king.

Doing nothing does not mean nothing happens.

Elijah hid in a cave on Mount Horeb where God broke into the prophet's self-pity and low view of himself by asking, 'What are you doing here?'[4] Believing in nothing does not lead to a life of content but to an emptying of it, until one day purpose disappears.

LIVING WATERS

Nestled within the book of Ezekiel there is a wonderful picture of hope and healing through the picture of moving water. The words describe a living water that overflows from the temple, symbolic of God's presence, which has the redemptive power to purify and renew everything.

The invitation of living waters that flows from God can rid the soul of infected thoughts and the disease of discontent. Jesus evokes this imagery to describe himself and to declare that he is the Messiah not long after his meeting with the woman at the well, whom he had asked for water.

Jesus stands up at a major festival and in a loud voice invites anyone who is spiritually thirsty to come to him and drink. He goes on to say that whoever believes in him will have rivers of living water flowing from within them.[5] His audience knew instantly from their Hebrew Bibles that flowing waters were symbolic of God's faithfulness and lasting provision for them.

Whenever life throws a curved ball, it always gives an opportunity for Jesus to declare himself as the living waters that comes to disrupt the deadness of sin, to allow his dynamic rule to continue to reign over us, and for his Holy Spirit to get our faith moving again.

WHERE EVERYTHING FLOWS, EVERYTHING LIVES

Jesus invites us to see himself as the holy waters that flow from God's heart to drench our souls and saturate our every thought and concern. His living waters also do another job. They begin to dilute our fears and anxieties, to rid us of those negative feelings that want to offer an alternative style of rulership over our lives.

Psychologists say that planned change is even more stressful than unplanned change, but we wouldn't think so when we are in the thick of it. That's because we will want to fight it or ignore it, but the one thing we cannot do is deny the change. This is why, when we try to stay in control of an unplanned change, we will see our stress levels and emotions rise.

We need a different attitude to see it through. One that listens, trusts and waits.

In times of unplanned change, we need to continue to welcome the flow of God's goodness in us to be able to accept our suffering and be assured that it has a place in his plan, even if it is not in our own. But this living water only flows where it is allowed to flow. We need to trust and surrender and not push and punish ourselves when we see no signs of movement.

The Holy Spirit comes only by invitation; but always by consent, never by coercion.

Jesus' invitation to us to come to himself as living waters points to how he will take a stagnant faith and renew us by stirring us up.

The Hebrew words we translate as Holy Spirit, *ruach ha-kodesh*, also means 'breath of Spirit'. He is a living force who is able to get anything to move again. When we welcome God's presence, he breathes his life over us to disturb the stagnant waters of our thoughts and emotions to re-oxygenate hope for ourselves. God's present is his presence over us, in us and around us.

This is how spiritual transformation continues in us. Change means something new is happening. It means some interruptions will be disruptions to help us see a new beginning. But as Richard Rohr suggests, it only happens 'not when something new begins, but when something old falls apart'.[6] And if we are being honest, not many of us know what needs changing until something new comes along to show us what's at work in us and what's not.

Stir It Up! 169

The word given to Ezekiel by the Lord speaks life into the deadness of the human experience:

> When I arrived there, I saw a great number of trees on each side of the river. He said to me, 'This water flows toward the eastern region and goes down into the Arabah, where it enters the Dead Sea. When it empties into the sea, the salty water there becomes fresh. Swarms of living creatures will live wherever the river flows. There will be large numbers of fish, because this water flows there and makes the salt water fresh; so where the river flows everything will live. Fishermen will stand along the shore; from En Gedi to En Eglaim there will be places for spreading nets. The fish will be of many kinds – like the fish of the Mediterranean Sea.'[7]

For the Jews it was a picture of a restored life out of the ruins of the once great city of Jerusalem, representing their once great faith. 'Where everything flows everything will live.'

It seems inconceivable that Jesus would not want to interrupt us. In fact, not to interrupt us would contradict his loving concern and faithfulness to us. I for one am grateful not to be left alone to stagnate in my own faith where I might be tempted to pick, choose and decide what I would like for myself without ever being challenged.

But God does something else. Living waters don't flow through us to move us but mix with us. Much like new water mixing with stagnant water, Jesus comes to share in our condition, to experience our suffering, sin and shame while breathing his resurrected life into us. He allows himself to be born into a broken world as fully God and fully human where he willingly mixes his deity with all the greediness, selfishness and brokenness of a seemingly lost cause.

Emma and I, along with one of our daughters who was twelve at the time, went for a lunch at a picturesque pub on the Orford estuary in Essex. By the side of the pub was a rough-and-ready wooden jetty that led down to the water with moored boats. After lunch when the tide was out, we decided to walk along it. Halfway down I thought it would be fun to dangle our daughter over the edge just holding her hands. Below her was a thick, oily, sludge-like mud with an unpleasant stench.

You can probably guess what happened next.

I suddenly realised I was at a tipping point and had to make a call. Do I let my daughter fall in so only one of us gets muddy – or do we both go in?

170   *Life, Interrupted*

Rest assured; I chose the latter. Saving myself was never really an option. We all find ourselves in positions where we get ourselves and the ones we love into messes. We call it sin – and it really is as simple as that. The good news is that Jesus does not stay distant from our messes but jumps in to save us and pull us out.

A HORROR STORY AND LOVE STORY ALL IN ONE

When I was at Sunday school, I used to have a bucolic picture of Jesus walking around Nazareth and Lake Galilee in a white robe that was forever immaculately clean. I thought that, much like Alex Guinness's clothing in the 1951 film, *The White Suit*, it never got dirty. Not even when he picked up dirt and mixed it with his spittle to heal a man of his blindness or when he slept rough or spent time in the desert being tempted by the devil.

The truth, however, is that his robes must have got absolutely filthy. How could they not? This is someone who had known muck and squalor since birth. This is the one born in a dirty stable in an over-crowded town. So I wonder, why do so many of us struggle with the following words of Paul the apostle? 'God made him who had no sin to be sin for us, so that in him we might become the righteousness of God.'[8]

The thought of Jesus being made 'sin for us' is an uncomfortable one, isn't it? But Paul is wanting to point us back to the horror of the cross with his 'big blue neon sign' statement, to remind us how Jesus allowed himself to be crucified surrounded by two thieves and the stench of rubbish outside the city wall. It is not a pleasant thought but then sin is not pleasant. I wonder sometimes whether, if we could actually smell our sin, we would repent that little bit quicker!

It makes the cross both a horror story and a love story. Its bad news is its good news. Jesus becoming sin is what saves us. On that terrible hill he began to turn our ashes to beauty, our mourning to joy and our heaviness into praise.

It is an act of love so profound that it can provoke only gratitude in us. It is why I make confession part of my daily prayer. It lifts me, making me clean each time, much like putting on a fresh white shirt. But it is also my constant reminder that I am a child of God who is lavished with the love of a doting Father. Let's now turn to look at another love story.

GET UP AND MOVE!

Jesus arrives at a pool in Jerusalem that resembles a hospital waiting-room. There are many disabled people around the water. Some are blind, others are lame or can't move at all. One man has been coming to the water for thirty-eight years. Like the others, he believes that the waters would be stirred by an angel of the Lord and the first one in would be healed. Unfortunately, because he is paralysed, he never beats the others to the water. Jesus has little time for this crazy superstition. He cuts to the chase and tells the man to move: 'Get up! Pick up your mat and walk.'[9]

Jesus interrupts the man's distorted way of looking for help in the wrong places and shows himself to be the only true living waters where people can find real hope and healing.

A few months into being ill with Covid-19, I was able to reflect with more coherence and clarity. I slowly became aware that this time was not the curse I had at my lowest points believed it to be. I had never stopped for so long or had so much time on my hands. My feelings oscillated from guilt to gratitude.

I began to review my fourteen years as a founding pastor of a wonderful and vibrant church plant. I gave thanks for Emma, who was able to lead the church at this time largely without my help, which I think was a revelation to us both.

I gave thanks to the highly dedicated and extraordinarily ebullient staff team, along with the faithful volunteer leaders who gave everything to keep the ministry of the church moving. This was no small thing as many of them had families to look after with the stress of home-schooling while trying to do a job also working from home.

I gave thanks for the ever-deepening care and sacrifice of the compassion programme team. The emergency food they served to local families and individuals in crisis became known as 'bags of hope'. In this same period, we also helped to launch a wider community initiative with local town councillors and other churches called 'Love Your Neighbour'. It helped isolated, housebound and vulnerable people with practical things such as shopping, meals and dog-walking.

But then God took me back to a memory from our sabbatical in 2018 when we were in Cincinnati, Ohio, with our friends, Dave and Anita Workman.

One evening Emma and I pondered on a conversation we had had with them. We had discussed the courage and conviction with which Dave had chosen to step down from leading the church before his time, because he saw the church was greying with him. We saw it as something that was sacrificial and risky, but we also saw God in his decision, along with Dave's obedience to do the will of the Father.

There was something that was beautifully servant-hearted about it. We reflected and prayed together that God would show us clearly when our time was up, and not when we thought we would like to go.

LETTING GO

Back in the present as I sat in my chair, I pondered what it would take for me to hand over the church we had pioneered and poured ourselves into. I had spoken to other leaders who had struggled to let go of their positions. Some struggled more than others because they saw it meant letting go of their identity. It would need to be something pretty big and life-changing, something maybe like a global pandemic!

For the whole of the church's life, I had worked continuously, bi-vocationally doing the work of two men, some said Laurel and Hardy, but it became evident as the church was growing that I could not continue as before, even if I got better. I was struck by something that Boise Vineyard's founding pastor, Tri Robinson, said: 'When a church gets to a certain size it can't just continue to scale up. It needs to become a different animal, it needs to change into something else altogether.'

The interruption of Covid-19 put my two demanding jobs into the spotlight. The Holy Spirit also graciously recalled those times when I was encouraged to keep going and not give up – and there were many – but he also showed me my weaknesses.

I began to see my limitations due to my time restraints and how they might affect the lives of others. The thought of hindering God's mission to transform many more lives, inside and outside the church, began to play on my heart. I had wanted to see the love of Jesus break into the lives of our community only for people to experience the same power of forgiveness and healing as I had myself.

But here's the thing: although Covid-19 had brought me to a standstill, my faith had not become stagnant as I had feared.

On the contrary, my 'time out' began to show me God's own view of my life. I saw signs of my soul being repaired after many years of the wear and tear of ministry. It even brought renewed hope for the things I was still desperate to see. But the biggest thing was seeing through the kindness of rest that God loved me just as I was.

Even though still ill and suffering with discomfort I enjoyed the days that followed, and became excited that God was speaking about the church's future, but it was becoming evident that it would not be with us. Meanwhile, Emma told me that she had been on her own journey with God and felt she was being told the same thing.

With each passing week we had an increasing sense that God was leading our thinking, and so we made the decision to lay down the church leadership – even though it meant firing ourselves and losing our financial security. Telling our board of trustees, staff and church was one of the hardest things we have ever had to do. I can't say we felt relief, but there was peace in the decision.

In some ways it was mad to hand our notice in and to find our successors during a global pandemic, but we believed God had spoken. I was reminded of Elijah on Mount Carmel who got his servants to douse the sacrifice with twelve large jars of water before seeing God send fire to consume the sacrifice.[10]

On some ways it felt we had doused our decision and made it harder for ourselves by trying to move at a time when many people were losing their jobs, furloughed or fearful of contemplating their next move. When the odds are stacked against us is exactly the place we may witness a miracle.

WE WILL KNOW IF WE ARE SUCCESSFUL ONLY IF WE HAVE SUCCESSORS

We always said from when our church first met in our living-room that we would know if this church has been successful only if we had successors. Only when we have made disciples and made leaders from disciples will we know that we have made a lasting difference.

The next year my health noticeably improved and we saw our replacements, Joel and Kady Taylor, arrive – all the way from San Francisco, although not without hiccups with visas and passports. But it wasn't so much a conclusion of a journey as a continuation of the same journey – just with different drivers.

My interruption had become a disruption, but God's focus had always been on what it had disrupted, not the disruption itself. I thought of Jesus healing a man with a withered hand on the Sabbath and how the Pharisees saw only the disrupter breaking their laws. The religious leaders totally missed the joy found in the disruption.[11]

Many people have said that they hope life doesn't go back to how it was before the pandemic. However, there are signs of this already happening. Maybe the cost of doing life differently is too high, as it is uncomfortable and unsettling to make a lasting habit. You can understand a longing for a familiar pattern, even if the old routine was far from perfect. But reverting could result in a lost opportunity to have a new adventure. And the older we get the more we are in danger of seizing fewer opportunities and choosing convenience over a fresh challenge.

FREEDOM!

We may want to be free from interference, but Paul the apostle says this is no freedom at all, just a form of slavery that burdens the soul with angst.[12]

In fact, our lives are anything but free when we are left to our own devices. We are a danger to ourselves when we think having limits robs us of our freedom and rights. It is limits that give us freedom from anxiety and fear. They provide us with healthy barriers to keep us safe in times of chaos and confusion.

Without interruptions, knowing this freedom would become an elusive experience. When something breaks in unexpectedly, we can draw upon who we are and why we were made. It will give us the confidence for how to act in that moment, an opportunity to choose to respond in faith and see an exterior force at work in our lives.

As St Augustine says, 'Do not go outside yourself. Return to yourself! The truth dwells within.'[13]

What does freedom look like for the person who puts their trust in God?

The best way I can explain it is simply to see it as a relationship with Jesus: something that is living, flowing and moves freely through our everyday words and actions. It gives us energy, informs the mind and stirs the heart. But one thing it cannot be is static, without vision or purpose.

INDIFFERENCE

St Ignatius understood freedom as something which starts from within. He advocated that to cope with the pressures of life we need to become indifferent to them, to be able to take or leave something and to discern whether it helps us to 'praise God, reverence, and serve God' (Spiritual Exercises 23).[14] Freedom is letting go of those things that remove us from loving God and others, and staying engaged with what he is doing in us.

So how do we do that, you may ask.

If you are anything like me, there will be plenty of times when we are pulled off course. But as I shared, it is not the disrupter that really pulls us off course as much as we think, it actually started with what has been disrupted. It could be our bad attitude to possessions, money, relationships, environmental issues, identity . . . take your pick!

Paul tells Timothy that godly contentment sees how 'we brought nothing into the world, and we can take nothing out of it'.[15] That means that nothing or no one belongs to us but all are gifts from God. It is how Job was able to say, 'Naked I came from my mother's womb, and naked I shall depart. The Lord gave and the Lord has taken away; may the name of the Lord be praised.'[16]

Gratitude in all circumstances is our greatest asset in learning indifference to interruptions. Nothing belongs to us, which means all things belong to God; and it is seeing everything as gifts from heaven that helps set the soul free to live well and enjoy Jesus.

Interruptions are a test of our indifference and are there to help us move on in faith. And we can see each one as an invitation for his 'living waters' to stir us up and breathe his Spirit into our soul.

In fact, each interruption is nothing less than an invitation to experience God's love in a new way and to grow closer to Jesus.

This means we won't have to fear becoming stagnant in our faith.

It means we can flourish even in grief and times of deep uncertainty.

The impossible has just become possible. And remember, even if you lower anxiety by just one notch, the world has already become a better place to live in.

INTERRUPTER

MEDITATE

Take a little time slowly to read Jesus' words in John's Gospel. Stop, pause, and reread as the Holy Spirit directs.

> You did not choose me, but I chose you and appointed you so that you might go and bear fruit – fruit that will last – and so that whatever you ask in my name the Father will give you.
>
> *John 15:16*

PONDER

- What is being stirred up in you?
- Where are you feeling stagnant in your faith? What is not moving for you? Do any emotions or spiritual passions feel as if they have stopped freely flowing?
- Sometimes our emotions towards Jesus are deadened by disappointments, so ask him to help you recall anything that may have brought you to this place. Have you encountered discouragement with how some prayers have not been answered in a way you would like?

PRAY

Invite his 'living waters' to ebb and flow into any of your meandering thoughts as you pray this prayer:

Through your waters of healing, Lord, cleanse me, replenish me and give me your peace.

Stir up in me a new passion for yourself and for your world.

Draw close and remind me of your overwhelming generosity, faithfulness, and unfailing love for me.

Fill me with your joy and hope as I trust in you so I may always overflow with hope by the power of the Holy Spirit.

Amen.

14 THE INTERRUPTION OF REST

There is no doubt this book would have got written a lot faster if I had not been interrupted. But I am not sure that would have been for the better.

Many things have vied for my attention since I started writing these words, such as weddings, funerals, Christmas, Easter, England winning the cricket against New Zealand, weekends, lunches, coffee, phone calls, Amazon delivery drivers, notifications on my computer and phone, and an abnormally large fly buzzing around in my study.

When writing *Huckleberry Finn*, Mark Twain allowed himself to be distracted for long periods of time. In the end it took him over eight years to complete his classic novel about a carefree, good-natured son of a vagabond. His interruptions were seven other books. So all things considered, I think I am probably doing okay.

It made me wonder though if too many interruptions 'kill the flow', much like a small child who is abruptly taken out of their imaginary world of play. I read somewhere that some children are neurologically wired to struggle when transitioning from one thing to another, such as playtime to bedtime. When a parent interrupts them, they will scream and kick. To the child it ruins *everything*, even when they are rubbing their watery eyes and falling over with tiredness.

"
AND NOW EXCUSE ME, WHILE I INTERRUPT MYSELF."
MURRAY WALKER,
F1 SPORTS
COMMENTATOR

"
BE STILL"
PSALM 46:10

This is how we can be as adults too. We become lost in what we are doing, whether it is good for us or not, but there always comes a point when we need to stop and move on.

But we know that accepting change is not always simple. Something in us will want to resist it until the thing that we are currently doing grinds to a painful halt through attrition or simple exhaustion.

WHEN TO LEAVE THE STAGE!

I have observed this many times over the years with church and business leaders who have struggled to let go as things grow or as they grow older. Sometimes it has taken the forced intrusion of illness or a loss of key staff or volunteer leaders to interrupt the illusion that we are meant to keep going. We might even catch ourselves saying, 'If I can just get over this next problem, everything will be fine and then I can think about stopping!'

While on sabbatical in the USA I spoke to a pastor in Ohio who told me that he had just returned from a month's sabbatical. I said, 'Only a month?' He took pains to tell me how difficult it was to leave the church for too long because it needed him. I asked how old he was, and he told me sixty-eight. I enquired if he had any succession plans in place.

'Oh yes', he said, 'My son will take over when he's ready.'

His son was in his mid-forties and had been his assistant pastor for several years.

Even the best-intentioned of us can struggle to trust God with an unknown future not least when everything is so familiar to us. It is a far easier option to 'soldier on' in an imperfect situation and stick to a cultivated routine, than to embrace the unknown. Even though the levels of our fruitfulness are diminishing we will continue to squeeze as much juice as we can out of our existing systems, rather than change our ways and take a chance planting a new orchard.

My wife and daughters joke that every shirt I buy is essentially the same one – blue, and sometimes with stripes, just to mix it up. Canadian author and coach, Carey Nieuhoff, confesses to a similar habit – and I am pretty sure we are far from the only two. You could say my tastes are conservative, but I am not about to change unless there is a global shortage of blue dye and, even then, I would find second-hand shirts – and have done so.

Nieuhoff notes that it is because our brain craves only what it knows and has experienced, which he suggests makes us liable to keep repeating established preferences unless something stops us.

The reason I often wear blue shirts is because I have had some success with them in the past. They have worked for me on a variety of different occasions, but the fact remains, as I have got older, I have become less adventurous in my fashion sense. At one point my daughters even introduced a rule that banned me from wearing shirts on Saturday.

The weekend interruption, which I hasten to add was monitored, forced me into rediscovering the world of T-shirts and hoodies, even though I am now stuck on white T-shirts but, hey, we are all a work in progress. Nieuhoff observes, 'The greatest enemy of your future success is always your current success.'[1]

So how do you embrace change without the screaming and kicking?

THE FUTURE'S BRIGHT

I have long admired the now defunct Orange mobile brand. In 1994 it launched its service with the refreshingly hopeful strapline: 'The future's bright, the future's orange.' It was a positive uplifting message, communicated with simplicity and confidence. It also did wonders for its sales to make it into what marketeers like to call a 'disrupter brand'. The message was clear: life is going to be better with every new connection you make.

It is a sentiment underlined all these years later with that convergence device we call the smart phone. And it's called smart for a reason. Because technology allows us to play curated non-stop streamed music, make video calls, send emails and texts, buy online, scroll social media and news and watch TV – whenever we like.

But it comes too with the neurosis of FOMO[2] which, if you haven't guessed by now, is exactly what tech companies trade on. They have us where they want us: in their pocket – and yours.

However, this portable tool of constant micro-interruptions is not the freedom we had in mind for ourselves. While it has lived up to its brand promise of giving us convenient living, quick information and easy access, the endless flow of non-stop communications can leave us languishing and wishing for deeper, more meaningful experiences.

Unwittingly, we have made ourselves slaves to a master of superficial connections. But we have also learnt to pacify our feelings by telling ourselves we are staying on top of everything going on. So how do we gauge what is important enough to continually allow our phones to interrupt our day? I mean, it is not that we aren't now aware of the mental health risks.

Fear of disconnection and the anxiety of being seen as absent are likely to be the main reasons why we put up very little resistance when our phones ping! You know this to be true. How many times have you broken away from an important conversation only to read that your package is eleven stops away? I bet you don't share that information. And the reason we don't share it is because we know it would make us look shallow and make the other person feel less important.

And yet, paradoxically, as I have tried to show in a previous chapter, we also need interruptions to break unhealthy patterns.

Something significant is needed to break the habit of non-productive activity. Not that we always recognise that is what is needed. This is because our blind spots will always stop us from seeing the true state of ourselves – and so it will need an intrusive external force to stop us in our tracks.

INTERRUPTING THE INTERRUPTERS

Depending on where we are at in life, we may be tempted to amend Orange's tagline and say, 'The future's uncertain, the future's grey'.

A piece of market research carried out on behalf of global brands showed Generation Z are both curious and cautious about what is ahead.[3] While older age groups may worry about health, pensions and pandemics, Generation Z's number one concern is climate change. Findings showed that they are more concerned about the planet's future than their own. It is perhaps no wonder veganism and ethical purchases are on the rise in this 16- to 24-year old age group as it is perceived to be just one area where they can have control over their lives.

The Interruption of Rest   181

And yet, the one substantial interruption they need from the uncertainties of a grey world is a transcendent hope.

It seems right now that the world is in a state of increasing chaos. As I write we are witnessing the biggest European war since 1945, which is having a serious effect on food and fuel supply chains. Trust in governments and institutions is at an all-time low. And closer to home, the problem with trust is no less.

In a televised political debate for the leadership of the Conservative Party, the audience was asked by the host if anyone thought politicians didn't lie. Not a single hand went up. With so much broken trust and uncertainty about the future, the anxious cry of a hurting humanity may be best found echoed in King David's prayer to God in his own time of unrest, 'Where does my help come from?'[4]

Mark Sayers points out that 'the world is moving into a grey zone phase as it shifts from a set of cultural assumptions caused by societal changes towards another place yet to be defined.'[5] The promise of secularism that humanity is always progressing and learning to be better without God has undoubtedly stalled in its progress.

You may have noticed that for all the breakthroughs in medical science, upgrades to our phones and campaigns around inclusivity and diversity we have not become any less angry, envious, greedy, hateful, manipulative, judgemental or selfish. We might now live longer, but the signs around us suggest our behaviour towards one another and ourselves has not improved as much as we had hoped.

Yes, there have been some amazing medical breakthroughs and I for one remain grateful for the NHS and my Covid-19 vaccine, but we still go to war. We still see powerful people imposing their will on others. We still see the rich getting richer and the poor getting poorer.

The human response in times of unrest has always been to start a movement; sometimes that comes with demonstrations and social reforms, other times with a bloody revolution, but the objective is always the same – to press reset.

DISRUPTED BY GOODNESS

George Orwell's famous allegorical novel, *Animal Farm*, was written at the end of the Second World War. It features a farmer who cruelly treats his farm animals, reminding us that pigs might be able to rise up and disrupt the order and bring balance but, given time, they will want to learn to walk and talk and wear exactly the same clothes as the farmer they have overthrown.[6]

The disrupters without a different kind of influence and role model easily become the next corrupted, which will then need another disrupter. Unless there is a more superior disrupter, one that is perfect in every way who is incorruptible and fully trustworthy, the patterns will keep reappearing. Nothing will change and humanity will remain stuck in its ways, having the same conversation.

Aristotle said educating the mind without educating the heart is no education at all, which tells us that if even the finest Greek minds of the day thought it was not enough, it is going to take something special to change the heart – or at least until there is an app for it!

Out of necessity, not just out of choice, we will need to have eyes wide open to new possibilities. It is here that heaven can break into the world and introduce an authentic Saviour of humanity, only this is also where our pride blinds us to wanting to seek answers beyond the proximity of our known human experiences.

This is why we will always need to be interrupted by supernatural goodness and be unable to be free enough in ourselves to seek it out. Only with the intrusion of divine hope through God's one and only Son can humanity really stand a chance of true reformation of the heart and a renewal of the mind.

This is what makes the words of Jesus such a powerful reminder that without his interruption there will always be limitations to our success: 'What good will it be for someone to gain the whole world, but forfeit their soul?'[7]

Without the constant involvement of a loving Creator God, our default switch will always want to regress to our own wisdom and knowledge. Until we can destroy the myth that becoming a better person is not a solo occupation, we will need to keep being interrupted. But why wait for God to interrupt us when we can interrupt ourselves? And there are several ways we can do this. First, by not talking so much!

THE INTERRUPTION OF SILENCE

A relationship with God is not something that allows us to put on autopilot. God wants us to be present to be able to enjoy freedom from anxious

The Interruption of Rest 183

thoughts and find singular contentment in his company. Silence found in him is a gift that brings a stillness within us but can also be a powerful voice that speaks into the noisiness of our days. It is anything but avoidance of a busy life, and more of a place to prepare for it. As the writer of Ecclesiastes reminds us, there is 'a time to be silent and a time to speak'.[8]

Isaiah says, we are to be like 'voices calling in the wilderness preparing the way for the Lord, making paths straight for him'.[9] It is our experiences forged in the desert that make us the best interrupters.

Ironically, in a world that has lost its power to communicate even though it chatters away constantly, it is the silence of God's company that gives our minds and hearts hope for ourselves and others. The stillness in us – which, as Ignatius of Loyola says, outwardly shows itself as indifference – is also something that communicates positively and is able to bring peace to others.

Over the years I have sat in many business and church meetings where some participants were too quick to express a view to show their value for being there (I have done it too), but some of the best remembered contributions were made when people chose not to speak first but to listen.

Henri Nouwen observes how silence is a quality of the heart that stays with us and in our conversation with others. It is also something that someone can take away with them. The learnt discipline is transportable, like a phone, and can speak in a way that words can't always do. Afterwards, it then allows us to return to the wilderness to be recharged. He notes, 'Words are the instrument of the present world, but silence is the mystery of the future world.'[10]

The interruption of silence offers us an invitation to stop and consider our next move, our next words, our next big decision, our next relationship. It is why retreats are such powerful times for leaders faced with tough and difficult choices, but the truth is we all need to learn the power of retreat to be able to advance. Silence is perhaps then the greatest interruption we will need as well as the one that we will often have little time for.

THE INTERRUPTION OF THE SABBATH

I talked early in this book about the incredible non-stop work rate of the leaf-cutter ant and how we are created to be different and to work within sensible limits of our ability. And if we can't, we deserved to be stopped. Apart from the fact that it is just plain exhausting!

And yet we so often imitate ant behaviour because we want to be productive in everything we do, even down to our quiet times and, unless we get something out of it, we feel disappointed or short-changed.

This is what makes the Sabbath such a welcome interrupter to our need always to want to be productive. The gift of time set aside by God has no expectation on us but to rest exclusively in his presence without agenda or motive.

That all sounds idyllic, but we know that there is real pressure to keeping a day set aside as different from the other six days. Because we have this need in us to be always productive, we hate 'wasting time'. We can be as easily driven in our rest as much as our work. If you can't sit on a beach without a phone, you will know what I mean.

God in his graciousness already knows of our pressures, which is why the Sabbath is not so much about being a good idea, but an instruction. It is gifted to us as a weapon of resistance against those things that want to keep us producing and consuming. Oh, and it is also good for mental health.

God's gift of the Sabbath, rooted in the story of creation in Genesis, comes between us and all those things in us that want to achieve, accomplish or win in life, but actually can have the perverse effect of enslaving us.

Western culture of productivity and consumerism, Walter Brueggemann observes, mirrors life under Pharoah, a man who carefully created an anxious restless system of work to satisfy his need for greater wealth and power.

The pyramids are a symbol of how success is built on a broad base of pain of misery to move upwardly to benefit only one master. It is a picture that is not dissimilar to what is happening in our world today where 1 per cent own 45 per cent of the world's personal wealth while nearly 3bn people have little or no wealth at all.[11]

It was only later in the silence of the wilderness that God instructed the now-free Israelites to rest as an antidote to the restlessness in the human mind. The wilderness became a place where Pharoah could not follow, but instead was left behind with his chariots and men sitting at the bottom of the Red Sea. Walter Brueggemann points to how the interruption of the Sabbath is an act of both resistance and alternative. First:

> It is resistance because it is a visible insistence that our lives are not defined by the production and consumption of commodity goods. Such an act of resistance requires enormous intentionality and communal reinforcement amid a barrage of seductive pressures from the insatiable insistencies of the market.[12]

Second, it also becomes the alternative to the demanding chattering presence of all those things going on in our lives that want to 'devour all our rest time' such as, dare I say, social media and online shopping.

The forced intrusion of observing the Sabbath in the Ten Commandments is an amazing gift that offers us time out from a system of life built on anxiety for a system of rest.[13] By interrupting ourselves, and our patterns that bring pressure, we are saying defiantly to a busy and unrelenting world that we will not be slaves of the anxious system. We will not be robbed of the freedom to rest in God – the One who has saved us from a life of enslaved thinking by always having to be productive. After all, as Walter Brueggemann concludes, 'The sabbath is not just the pause that refreshes. It is the pause that transforms.'[14]

THE INTERRUPTION OF WISDOM

From a place of rest, we will also be equipped to seek what is best or, as James the brother of Jesus calls it, wisdom from heaven. A wisdom that is 'peace-loving, considerate, submissive, full of mercy and good fruit, impartial and sincere'.[15]

I find it more than a note of interest that throughout the Bible God never apologises for intruding into anyone's life. Neither does he apologise when something else interrupts it. It is either a great omission or an admission that something else is going on behind our backs.

There are many times in the Bible when life for God's servants looks at best grey. Life can feel unfair or, worse still, that God doesn't care. But it is because God does care that things are allowed to affect us, which I know can sound like a strange kind of love, but bear with me here.

It is under the grey skies in a storm while in the boat on the water that character gets formed, not on dry land. The sanctity and purpose of life is fully appreciated when it is under threat, when we have no control and no one else can save us. It is in the place of no answers that Jesus likes to reveal himself as Lord over storms.

The image of Jesus being in the boat with his distressed disciples on the Sea of Galilee is a comfort to us not because he has the power to calm the storm, but because it brings greater clarity to understanding himself, as well as ourselves in the process.

We see Jesus on the Galilean Sea interrupting the storm clouds for blues skies to return, bringing peace into a time of uncertainty and fear. However, notice that Jesus never promises there will not be future storms. It will take more than one storm in life, one crisis, one upset to help us create a picture of who God is and how he loves to be able to live in a life totally surrendered to him.

Without the ongoing experience of grace encounters, my hunch is that we would only end up becoming insufferable to others, devaluing anything good that is in us.

Take Joseph. He was a privileged teenager living at home as the favourite son, while his brothers were out every day working hard in the fields. But his God-given gift to dream created jealousy in his brothers, who then sold him into Egyptian slavery.

His perfect life was interrupted by 17 years serving in a demanding Egyptian household, along with a life sentence in prison after a false accusation of rape. He would be middle-aged, around 41, before he experienced a privileged life again. Not because he rose to become the second most powerful person in Egypt after Pharoah, but because God showed favour and used him to save the whole of Israel. In fact, doubly privileged because he was also restored to his family.

In prolonged grey times, it was hard to see any good come out of disruption, but Joseph continued to trust God. In periods of uncertainty, we may want to question the words of Jeremiah who speaks of a loving God who tells us of his plans for us to prosper, not to harm us and to give us a hope and future.[16]

All things do work for the good of those who love God, but in times of immense pressure when doubts occur, we will need to constantly remind ourselves that the more we face our enemies – whether they are envy, greed, self-ambition, anger or ambivalence – the more opportunity we have to overcome and be transformed in Jesus' likeness. With each battle a little bit more of my old self has the opportunity to die for the new self to emerge.

Whether it is in a storm on a Galilean Sea or in a prison cell, this is where God clarifies his call on our lives. It is in the irritation of our interruptions that I find that God loves to reveal his glory.

FOR TRANSITIONS TO SIT WELL, KNOW WHERE YOU STAND

To be able to move on positively in times of unplanned distractions is to see the future as bright. Through the hope that lives in us, interruptions can be transformed from angst-ridden obstacles into grace-filled opportunities by us believing that God already has a plan to see us through them.

God is always present and by learning to remain in him with joyful hearts and prayer-filled lives, we can press on armed with confidence and assurance.

The promises made by Jesus profoundly live on in every age through each world disaster, economic downturn, war, famine or global pandemic. Jesus declares we will not perish but have everlasting life.[17] We will be with him in paradise where a new heaven and earth await us, along with new bodies because Immanuel – God with us – is for us.

I have concluded that it is not interruptions that are difficult, but life itself. Maybe a better place to look first is not at the interruption but what is being interrupted in us.

THE PROBLEM AS THE OPPORTUNITY

Whenever our church staff encountered problems, I told them to the point of boredom how every problem is an opportunity to do things differently.

The pandemic was one problem that became an opportunity. Many churches, much like ours, had their services and midweek programmes disrupted, but this led to the emergence of online services and new initiatives. In the absence of in-person services we saw many people come to church for the first time through our YouTube channel. We heard of people watching our online services and being healed. Our compassion programme caught the eye of the authorities, and we were offered large sums of money to reach more people in our community who were isolated and suffering because of the pandemic. Total strangers began to get in touch with us and asked to come on the next Alpha course. The problem became our greatest opportunity.

But it didn't stop there.

Many church leaders began to say how the pandemic was possibly a once-in-a-lifetime opportunity to reset the course of the church. We began to feel excited.

Beyond the initial shock of a loss of those things that we had ploughed our prayers, energy and time into, we began to embrace the opportunity as a legitimate reason to stop and review what was actually going on within our churches, not least within ourselves.

We shared together how it made it easier to end a ministry that had passed its 'sell by date' some time ago but we had been too afraid to act for fear of hurting feelings.

It also gave us time to dream. We became animated because we suddenly saw opportunities that our schedules previously hadn't allowed for. We saw new ways to reach our communities.

It was as if we had been unshackled from the constraints of a well-cultivated programme of activities that we had designed to keep the show on the road. We had subconsciously bought into the idea that a successful church is a busy, buzzing church, when really that was just a wearisome model that creates more work than rest. An additional place we commute to and not commune with.

Perversely within the ashes of lost lives to Covid-19, the disruption has seen new shoots appear. It is as if we have been given another opportunity and the Holy Spirit is able to rewild the church. The forced rest from busy church programmes and weekly routines might have been received with some screaming and kicking, everything does feel a little bit different. Something has changed, but it might take us a while to figure out what it is.

INTERRUPTER

FIND YOUR RESTING PLACE

Is there a place you can go to be alone, to gather your thoughts and talk intimately with Jesus? Somewhere to ask questions, cry and laugh with him? Jesus himself used an olive grove garden to be alone with his Father. My 'Gethsemane' is the common at the back of my house in Guildford. Where are your pathways of peace?

Consider this week finding your own 'garden' to walk and be alone with Jesus. He has already promised to meet you there. Psalm 91:1 says, 'Whoever dwells in the shelter of the Most High will rest in the shadow of the Almighty.' Go find your resting place.

AN ANCIENT PRAYER OF ST COLUMBA (AD 521–97)

Alone with none but thee, my God,
I journey on my way.
What need I fear when thou art near,
O King of night and day?
More safe am I within thy hand
Than if a host should round me stand.[18]

EPILOGUE

HOLY INTERRUPTIONS

In the middle of a record-breaking summer heatwave, I decided to tidy up my study. Digging around the back of my desk, a place that time had forgotten, I came across a pile of magazines that had collected no small amount of dust and dirt. They featured a monthly column that I had written on various occasions. I thumbed through some of the old issues, just to remind myself of the variety of topics, and stopped at December's edition. Maybe even subconsciously I thought it might cool me down a little, I don't know.

My column spoke about how heavy snow was forecast and how I needed to be at a meeting in Witney, the other side of Oxford. In preparation for my journey, I had remembered my father's advice and packed the car with a blanket, shovel, torch, jump leads and, for some reason, a family-sized packet of Minstrels. If there was to be any disruption on the journey, I would at least have chocolate to see me through the ordeal.

While munching through breakfast, I began to hear reports on the radio of trains being cancelled and motorways closing. It was at this point that Emma tried to dissuade me from going and asked what meeting was so important that it was worth me risking being stranded or having an accident. But no bit of snow was going to stop me. Man against the elements, and all that stuff!

A little while later it was announced that all schools were closing. Our daughters were of

> "EACH DAY IS A NEW BEGINNING.
>
> I KNOW THAT THE ONLY WAY TO LIVE MY LIFE
>
> IS TO TRY TO DO WHAT IS RIGHT, TO TAKE THE LONG VIEW,
>
> TO GIVE OF MY BEST IN ALL THAT THE DAY BRINGS,
>
> AND TO PUT MY TRUST IN GOD!"
> QUEEN ELIZABETH II[1]

course ecstatic. They then leapt up from the table and quickly rushed upstairs to change out of their school uniforms. It was clear they now had something else on their minds.

But it was in the chaos of a snowy winter morning that I very nearly missed out on the disruption.

In the next hour the snow got heavier and in the end someone wiser than me decided to cancel the meeting. A part of me was disappointed, regardless of being ready for all eventualities with my large bag of Minstrels, but it was in this moment I was given a precious and unexpected gift: I got a chance to stay home and make a snowman with my children.

The funny thing about snow is that we either see it as a nuisance or something beautiful, depending on our plans and what is ahead of us.

And even though snow is cold it is also beautiful. As I watched the snowflakes knock against our windows, I moved closer and began to see just how delicate and different each one was.

This up-close experience is something we will see only if we voluntarily stop and become attentive, but most times it seems for this to happen will need rather a disruption. If only we didn't have to wait to be interrupted and could find our own reason to stop!

HOLY MOMENTS NOT TO BE MISSED

We should not be surprised if an interruption is the thing that God will use to speak to whatever most needs addressing in us. For this reason, we might want to see them as holy interruptions – gracious intrusions that help encounter God's presence up close to be able to unlearn wrong ways. A place to stop and breathe during the unrelenting daily pressure of modern life.

Seeing the interruption as holy could just be our greatest resistance against a pharaoh of anxious productivity, which looks to rob us of our joy and freedom. A pause that supports the cause and works for good. Let's remind ourselves again of Jesus' fear-stopping, heart-warming words: 'Look at the birds of the air; they do not sow or reap or store away in barns, and yet your heavenly Father feeds them. Are you not much more valuable than they? Can any one of you by worrying add a single hour to your life?'[2]

Epilogue

Jesus disrupts our everyday concerns to bring us a timeless reassurance that our purpose can look different. Whatever is the destination of our thoughts and actions, it is resting in the uninterruptable truth of Jesus' words that will help to start to draw us back towards what is really important and of value. And that starts by being open to change, not trying to control it.

Interruptions are not there just to get through or go round, but something to experience and grow in, not least in our understanding of God's love and provision for us. Maturity can come only by letting go and surrendering something of high value. Only then will we have the chance of owning something of infinitely more value.

CONTINUITY IS NOT ALWAYS THE THING WE NEED, EVEN WHEN IT IS THE THING WE WANT

The God who disrupted the darkness at creation needs our continual permission to disrupt any darkness still living in us. And we know that seldom will the disruption be convenient or without discomfort. At these times, as Brother Andrew, founder of Open Doors has said, 'Don't curse the darkness, light a candle.'[3]

Invite God into your disruption, invite his light to work on your shadows. These may be the things in your character that you would rather others did not see. The things that affect your mood when you find yourself not in control, and cause you stress and anxiety.

We can guarantee there will be many battles of the will, times of humiliation, much failure, seasons of brokenness and uncertainty, but all can be used to help us find our way to hope and healing, and a greater revelation of God's love for us. Only in the times of 'unscheduled testing' can we hope to build a resilient faith strong enough to resist whatever lies ahead of us.

An interruption can also become the illumination to reveal the true condition of the world and its values, to lead out of false thinking into the joyful freeing experience of undeserved grace.

It is my prayer for you as you have read this book to discover with wonder how interruptions can be opportunities for God to reveal just how much he loves us. Because without him, quite frankly, the discomfort of continual disruptions is, well, like a leadless pencil – pointless! If not totally unbearable.

194 *Epilogue*

The poet W.H. Auden spoke of the interruption of an untimely death that brought him inconsolable grief: 'Stop all the clocks, cut off the telephone/Prevent the dog from barking with a juicy bone.' It is a grim picture of the agony of a faithless soul. He finishes with the deadening words, 'For nothing now can ever come to any good.'[4]

For the follower of Jesus, there will of course be times when the bigger interruptions confuse us and leave us asking, why? But this is where faith says, 'I do believe; help me overcome my unbelief!'[5]

However, to downgrade them as meaningless distractions is to miss out on something more profoundly transformative happening to our soul.

The words of W.H. Auden might ring true were it not for the permanency of hope given through the power of the cross and resurrection.

If hope did not rise in Jesus and we were left with the darkness of Good Friday, it would be foolish to believe in the uninterruptible plan that God has for our lives. We would be right to see it simply as a random collection of purposeless obtrusions that shape habits and dictate decisions.

Furthermore, it would mean each twist and turn has the power to keep us captive through anxiety and fear with an uncertain future. Each one miserably filled with a fateful attitude of 'Well, that's just life!'

But this is not our story.

This is not our destiny, thankfully.

Anything that breaks into our lives and seeks attention always holds an opportunity to reveal the resurrected hope that is at work within us, which I have found nine times out of ten starts with a change in character caused by a change in circumstances. But even if our circumstances do not change, the invitation is to not scream and kick. It is to stop and notice God close up, like the delicate designs of a snowflake.

Darkness was never our disrupter but is always the disrupted. God was always, and is, in control. His invitation to us is to see the disturbance of the darkness as an act of supreme love and to walk in his light.

Our first step is to seek the kingdom of God and his righteousness and to allow everything else to follow it; to experience God's mind with the renewal of our own to inform human understanding.

Epilogue   195

THERE IS NO SUCH THING AS A COMFORTABLE LIFE

A comfortable life is a myth. Whoever we are, whatever we have made of ourselves, interruptions will always turn up to challenge us. Some, of course, will be very welcome, like a cup of coffee appearing at our side, but others will rock our world. They will force us to question, cause us to doubt, upset our ideas about our faith and God himself. But the incredibly good news is, hope always brings comfort. It breaks up the clouds to allow the light to pour in.

There is always an invitation to address the condition of our soul and to lean into God's understanding through the welcoming of his presence into every situation by his Holy Spirit. He will help us to remember that all interruptions, like the Sabbath breaking into the week, can be holy and redemptive to bring spiritual wellbeing.

At the end of the day, I am just a coach, you are the one running your race. You are the one who needs to look out for you.

But you can start by not seeing each upset as a reason to quit but to get better, an opportunity to reset your stopwatch, check your trainers and go again. 'Run in such a way as to get the prize.'[6]

Meanwhile find those living waters, those streams of renewal to stop and catch your breath. Be refreshed by the one who gave everything for us to be free – Jesus. By his wounds we are healed of our wrong decisions and poor choices.

So no more interruptions from me.

I will leave you with the words from a wonderful old and familiar hymn. I encourage you to make it your prayer today and let it minister its sweetness to your soul.

O Breath of love, come breathe within us,

Renewing thought and will and heart;

Come, love of Christ, afresh to win us,

Revive your church in every part!

O Wind of God, come bend us, break us

till humbly we confess our need;

Then, in your tenderness remake us,

Revive, restore – for this we plead.[7]

Acknowledgements

Writing a book can be like putting on your Sunday best. You try to look smart, but somehow you know you're not kidding anyone. So I can be only myself – a spiritual scruffbag conveying thoughts with an internal hope they might help see a little more change in us.

I suspect too it could have been written a little better, but it also could have gone a lot worse – had it not been for the love and support of some truly wonderful people around me. A debt of thanks to Eddie Lyle, who first inspired me to get my pen out in January 2020. Friendship is one thing, honesty in friendship is quite another.

It is with gratitude that I want to thank the amazing community that is Stour Valley Vineyard Church, whose own re-storied lives have kept me company while writing much of it. Also, profound thanks to my many friends at Open Doors whose unyielding commitment to serve the persecuted church has only helped to fuel my determination to get it done.

Paul the apostle showed how writing in times of personal difficulty needs sacrifice to advance the gospel (Phil. 1:12). But without friends the task becomes a million times harder, and while there are too many to name, I do need to mention Chris and Maggie Parsons and Dave and Anita Workman whose wisdom, godly influence and outward-focused lifestyle is second to none. And to my closest companions in life for over forty years who have always been there and helped me, most importantly, not to take myself too seriously: Markie Mark, Stevie Sticks and Trevor 'the colonel'.

Special thanks to Rick and Lulu Williams who first took a risk with a fresh-faced graduate and to Steve Fenning for walking the road with me. It would also be remiss of me not to especially thank Pete and

Sammy Greig and the family at Emmaus Road for welcoming us with such open arms and for being the real deal.

To the team at Authentic Media, I simply want to say a heartfelt thank you for helping to make this book happen. Your support and understanding through each fresh interruption has only made me more grateful for you all and for what we have achieved together.

LAST AND NOT LEAST . . .

Emma, what can I say? You are more than a wife in Proverbs, you are my best friend. Thank you for reading and rereading my words again and again and again. Without your encouragement, this book might have just fizzled out and been forgotten by Monday lunchtime. We trust and obey, for there's no other way.

About the Author

Andrew Stewart-Darling has spent nearly thirty years in pastoral ministry with Vineyard Churches UK & Ireland and the Church of England. He received a degree from London School of Theology before joining staff at Riverside Vineyard in west London. He later helped to establish All Souls, an Anglican church plant in Twickenham, Middlesex, and founded Stour Valley Vineyard Church in Sudbury, south Suffolk, along with Storehouse, the town's foodbank.

Over the years Andrew has felt called to stay working bi-vocationally in marketing and advertising and has held the positions of creative director and group strategy director before becoming a consultant.

Andrew and his wife Emma were Area Leaders for Vineyard Churches in East Anglia, and later became part of the 24-7 Prayer movement. Their church ran the first 24-7 Prayer Room in Suffolk. They handed over the leadership of the church in 2021 and have since moved to Guildford to become part of Emmaus Road.

As part of his vision to see interrupted leadership, Andrew spends part of his time mentoring church leaders, as well as providing strategy and training in mostly Christian organisations.

To interrupt Andrew and start a conversation, you can find him on social media or in a café somewhere in Guildford in search of the perfect Flat White.

Notes

INTRODUCTION

[1] Job 33:4.

[2] Taken from a scene in the film, *The Darkest Hour* (Perfect World Pictures, 2017). The War Cabinet discusses whether it is best to surrender with terms to Adolf Hitler or to fight on, knowing it could be the end of the British Empire.

[3] John 3:27.

[4] Peter Scazzero, *Emotionally Healthy Spirituality* (Grand Rapids, MI: Zondervan, 2006), pp. 148–9.

1 – MORE THAN A BLIP

[1] Brother Bernard, *Open to God* (London: Fount, 1986), p. 144.

[2] Luke 10:34.

[3] We can get distracted by the high ages of some people in the Old Testament, but in ancient Mesopotamian culture it wouldn't be unusual to add years to a person's age to honour them. Noah's grandfather Methuselah was said to have lived 969 years (Gen. 5:27). However, one of the highest ages given before the great flood was to the Sumerian king in Eriduf, Alumin, who ruled some glorious 28,800 years. It was not an age to be taken literally, but to be seen as an honour bestowed upon someone who was considered great or notable.

[4] Hob. 11:7.

[5] C.S. Lewis, *The Collected Letters of CS Lewis, Volume II: Family Letters 1905-1931* (London: HarperCollins, 2010). © Copyright 2004 CS Lewis Pte Ltd. Extract used with permission.

2 – THINGS THAT GO BUMP!

[1] Quote from 'Lilith' by George McDonald, found in *The Collected Works of C.S. Lewis: The Pilgrim's Regress* (Nashville, TN: Thomas Nelson, 1996), p. 123.

[2] Quote from the seventeenth-century English poet, John Pomfret, 'Reason' from *Oxford Book of Quotations* (Oxford: Oxford University Press, 1989), p. 375.

[3] John Maxwell comments on the Roman emperor Julius Caesar's work, *Di Bello Civili*, quoted in *The 15 Invaluable Laws of Growth: Live Them and Reach Your Potential* (London: Hachette UK, 2012).

[4] Lewis Carroll, *Alice's Adventures in Wonderland* (Macmillan).

[5] William Morris, *The Well at The World's End: Volume I* (Maryland: Wildside Press, 2000).

[6] Matt. 7:7.

[7] Rev. 3:7–8.

[8] Gen. 28:17.

[9] Quoted from an article by Tom Whipple: 'Globalisation of Gloom Means We're All Miserable Now', *The Times* (Tuesday 28 March 2023).

[10] https://nypost.com/2018/05/02/new-york-really-is-the-city-that-never-sleeps/# (accessed 9 Nov. 2023).

[11] Jenevieve Treadwell, 'Burn Out Britain' research report, *Onward* (2023), p. 38.

[12] Gen. 1:31.

[13] John 3:16 (my italics).

3 – STOP ME IF YOU THINK YOU HAVE HEARD THIS ONE BEFORE

[1] Frederick Buechner, *The Hungering Dark* (New York: Seabury Press, 1969), p. 72.

[2] John 10:10.

[3] Market data supplied by App Annie who reported that, in 2021, 230 billion new apps were downloaded across the world. https://www.appannie.com/en/insights/market-data/state-of-mobile-2022/ (accessed 9 Nov 2023).

4. Ps. 139:23.
5. Dietrich Bonhoeffer, *Life Together* (New York: HarperCollins, 1954), p. 8.
6. Eccl. 3:11.
7. Linda Ellis and Mac Anderson, *Dash: Making a Difference with Your Life from Beginning to End* (Nashville: Thomas Nelson, 2012), p. 13.
8. Mark Batterson, *Wild Goose Chase* (Colorado: Multnomah, 2008), p. 16.
9. John 10:10.
10. Brother Andrew is the late founder of Open Doors, a global Christian ministry which serves persecuted Christians around the world.
11. Phil. 3:14.
12. Col. 2:6–7.
13. John Maxwell, *The 15 Invaluable Laws of Growth: Live Them and Reach Your Potential* (London: Hachette UK, 2012).

4 – GIVE YOURSELF A BREAK

1. https://www.fws.gov/story/2016-03/5-fascinating-facts-about-leaf-cutter-ants (accessed 10 Nov. 2023).
2. © Justin Welby, 2016, *Dethroning Mammon* (London: Bloomsbury Continuum, an imprint of Bloomsbury Publishing Plc), p. 11. Used with permission.
3. Welby, *Dethroning Mammon*, p. 11.
4. Prov. 29:18, KJV.
5. Quoted in *The Complete Mystical Works of Meister Eckhart* (trans. Maurice O'C. Walsche; New York: Crossroad, 2009).
6. https://www.mynd.uk/the-mynd-pod (accessed 10 Oct. 2023).
7. Isa. 61:1.
8. Josh. 1:9.
9. Luke 12:7.
10. Rom. 8:1.
11. Dietrich Bonhoeffer, *Letters and Papers from Prison* (London: SCM, 1971).

5 – USE YOUR IMAGINATION!

[1] Part of a speech President Kennedy delivered on urgent national needs to the Joint Session of Congress on 25 May 1961.

[2] Mark 9:24.

[3] Alfred Lord Tennyson, *All Things Will Die*.

[4] Eccl. 3:1–2.

[5] Prov. 28:19.

[6] Gen. 37:9.

[7] A.W. Tozer, *The Knowledge of the Holy* (Kent: STL Books, 1984), p.16.

[8] Gen. 17.

[9] Stanley C. Griffin, *A Forgotten Revival: East Anglia and NE Scotland – 1921* (Kent: Day One, 1992), p. 16.

[10] Leo Burnett started life selling apples in a market in Chicago before forming an advertising agency. His words, I believe, continue to be used today at staff inductions. A hand reaching for the stars used also to appear in its worldwide branding until it was replaced by his signature.

[11] The *Boy's Own Paper* first appeared in 1878 and had at its core the vision to instil Christian values into schoolchildren, mainly to those in Britain's public schools it must be said. It feted the success of empire and was muscular in tone. Many of its social/ moral values would of course not survive today's post-colonial, twenty-first-century culture, but it gives us a fascinating snapshot into 'Christian Britain'.

[12] Luke 1:18.

[13] Quoted in https://www.washingtonpost.com/archive/lifestyle/ 1980/10/27/children-in-a-world-of-fantasy/85aed41b-c4e8- 4fbd-846e-f7e7f65a5d9d/ (accessed 10 Oct. 2023).

[14] 1 Cor. 12:4.

[15] Acts 2:17.

[16] Mark 9:23–4.

6 – HOW TO BE AN EVERYDAY ORDINARY HERO

[1] Phil. 4:13.

[2] Ps. 139:14.

3   Derek Kidner, *Psalms 73–150* (London: Inter-Varsity Press, 1975), p. 502.

4   Grant Morrison, *Supergods: What Masked Vigilantes, Miraculous Mutants, and a Sun God from Smallville Can Teach Us about Being Human* (New York: Random House, 2011), p. 11.

5   Morrison, *Supergods*, p. 11.

6   Eph. 5:8.

7   Luke 2:11.

8   Friedrich Nietzsche and R.J. Hollingdale, *Thus Spoke Zarathustra* (London: Penguin Classics), 1974. The German philosopher sets out the idea of 'superman' in the introduction of the book to argue that the meaning of life is not found being under authority of God or any other authority but in individual freedom.

9   2 Cor. 12:9–11.

10   Jules Feiffer, *The Great Comic Book Heroes* (New York: Double-day, 1968). Sadly, now out of print and has been for thirty years.

11   Judg. 13:3–5.

12   Judg. 13:25.

13   Richard Foster, *Money, Sex and Power* (London: Hodder & Stoughton, 1985), p. 135.

14   Richard Rohr, *Immortal Diamond* (London: SPCK, 2013), p. 43.

15   Judg. 16:30.

16   John 12:24.

17   Matt. 12:21.

18   Julian of Norwich, *Showings*, Chapter 22 (Short text) (trans. Edmund Colledge and James Walsh; Mahwah: Paulist Press, 1978), p. 164.

19   Billy Graham quotes from BrainyQuote.com, BrainyMedia Inc., 2023. https://www.brainyquote.com/quotes/billy_graham_161989 (accessed 10 Nov. 2023).

20   Eugene Peterson, *The Contemplative Pastor* (Grand Rapids, MI: Eerdmans, 1989), p. 15.

21   Blaise Pascal, *Selected Readings from Blaise Pascal* (ed. with introduction by Robert Van de Weyer; Hunt & Thorpe, 1991), p. 52.

22   Arthur C. Brookes, *From Strength to Strength* (London: Green Tree, 2023), p. 85.

7 – MAY I STOP YOU RIGHT THERE?

[1] St Augustine, *Confessions* (trans. Benigus O'Rourke; London: Darton, Longman & Todd, 2013), p. 13.

[2] Matt. 6:33.

[3] Excerpt from 'The Sayings of the Desert Fathers': *The Apophthegmata Patrum: The Alphabetic Collection* by Benedicta Ward, SLG, trans. CS 59 (Collegeville, MN: Cistercian Publications, 1975), p. 32. Used by permission of Liturgical Press. All rights reserved.

[4] See Phil. 4:6.

[5] See Ps. 23:2.

[6] Brother Andrew, *And God Changed His Mind: Because His People Prayed* (London: Harper Collins, 1991).

[7] Jas 3:17.

[8] Tom Kington, 'I'm No Saint, Pope Admits in Chat Show Appearance' (*The Times*, 7 Feb. 2022).

[9] Martin Laird, from foreword to St Augustine, *Confessions*.

[10] St Augustine, *Confessions*, p. 91.

[11] Jer. 6:13.

[12] St Augustine, *Confessions*, p. 143.

[13] Mark 10:17.

[14] Mark 10:21.

[15] James R. Edwards, *The Gospel According to Mark* (Grand Rapids, MI: Eerdmans, 2002), p. 309.

[16] Frederick Buechner, *The Hungering Dark* (New York: Seabury Press, 1969), pp. 31–2.

[17] Luke 8:17.

8 – TO BE CONTINUED . . .

[1] Fyodor Dostoevsky, *Crime and Punishment* (London: Penguin Classics, 2003).

[2] David Hillman and Adam Phillips, *The Book of Interruptions* (Switzerland: Peter Lang AG, 2007), p. 8.

[3] Gen. 30:43.

[4] Gen. 46:30.

[5] John 10:10.

206   *Notes*

[6] John 19:30.

[7] Gen. 1:1.

[8] Lam. 3:22–3.

[9] John 1:5.

[10] Donald Miller, *A Million Miles in a Thousand Years* (Nashville, TN: Thomas Nelson, 2009), p. 100.

[11] Farming Community Network supports farmers and their families within the farming community, providing a confidential helpline. It offers pastoral and practical support through its army of amazing volunteers. Over 6,000 people a year in the UK received help.

[12] Jonah 1:1–2.

[13] Gen. 10:11.

[14] C.S. Lewis, *The Weight of Glory* (London: HarperCollins, 2013). © Copyright 1949 CS Lewis Pte Ltd. Extract used with permission.

[15] https://jesuitinstitute.org/Pages/Prayers.htm (accessed 11 Nov. 2023).

[16] Matt. 19:26.

[17] John Bunyan, *The Pilgrim's Progress* (Oxford: Oxford Paperbacks, 1984).

[18] 1 Cor. 9:24.

[19] 1 John 4:19.

[20] Quoted by Margaret Hebblethwaite, *The Way of St Ignatius: Finding God in All Things* (London: Fount, 1987), p. 16.

9 – WET FEET

[1] Quoted in *The Times* (Wed. 25 May 2022).

[2] Lam. 3:21–3, esv.

[3] Brother Lawrence, *The Practice of the Presence of God* (trans. E.M. Blaiklock; London: Hodder & Stoughton, 1996), p. 24.

[4] Alan Jones, *Soul Making* (New York: Seabury Press, 1974), pp. 73–85.

[5] Rowan Williams, *Silence and Honey Cakes: The Wisdom of the Desert* (Oxford: Lion Hudson, 2004), pp. 79–80.

[6] Josh. 4:20–24.

[7] Prov. 20:5–6.

[8] 1 John 3:19.

Notes   207

[9]   1 John 3:20.
[10] 1 John 3:21–2.
[11] Margaret Hebblethwaite, *The Way of St Ignatius: Finding God in All Things* (London: Fount, 1987), p. 114.
[12] Richard Rohr, *Falling Upward* (London: SPCK, 2012), p. 157.
[13] John Mark Comer, *Live No Lies* (London: SPCK, 2021).

10 – YOU IN THE FUTURE

[1]   St Augustine, *Confessions* (trans. Benigus O'Rourke; London: Darton, Longman & Todd, 2014), p. 313.
[2]   Youth With a Mission (YWAM) was founded by Loren Cunningham in 1960 and has become a large global movement of Christians from many cultures, age groups and Christian traditions, dedicated to serving Jesus throughout the world. https://ywam.org.
[3]   C.S. Lewis, *The Weight of Glory* (London: HarperCollins, 2013). © Copyright 1949 CS Lewis Pte Ltd. Extract used with permission.
[4]   Mark 9:21–3.
[5]   Acts 2:42.
[6]   Matt. 28:19.
[7]   1 Thess. 5:16–18.
[8]   Heb. 10:24–5.
[9]   Acts 2:44.
[10] Peter Scazerro, *Emotionally Healthy Spirituality* (Grand Rapids, MI: Zondervan, 2014), p. 18.
[11] Eph. 4:22, CEV.
[12] Eph. 4:23–4, CEV.
[13] Prov. 26:11.
[14] Gal. 6:7–8.
[15] Romans 13:11.
[16] Romans 13:11–14, MSG.
[17] 1 Pet. 5:8, NLT.
[18] Matt. 6:24.
[19] Matt. 26:41.
[20] Quoted by St Niodemos the Hagiorite in Part 2, Chapter 2, of his *Concerning Frequent Communion*, p. 169.
[21] 2 Cor. 4:12,16.

208 Notes

[22] J.R.R. Tolkien, *The Fellowship of the Ring* (London: HarperCollins, 1954).

[23] R. Alan Cole, *Galatians* (Grand Rapids, MI: IVP, 1991), p. 228.

[24] 1 Pet. 5:8.

[25] 1 John 4:8.

11 – WHAT DIFFERENCE DOES IT MAKE?

[1] C.S. Lewis, *The Weight of Glory* (London: HarperCollins, 2013). © Copyright 1949 CS Lewis Pte Ltd. Extract used with permission.

[2] Rom. 8:37.

[3] An international evangelistic ministry which is now known in the UK as Good News for Everyone.

[4] John 4:12.

[5] Statistics taken from the Ministry of Justice: https://www.gov.uk/government/statistics/proven-reoffending-statistics-october-to-december-2019/proven-reoffending-statistics-october-to-december-2019#statisticians-comment.

[6] Mark Lutz, *What is Wrong with People?* (Minneapolis: Mill City Press, 2015), pp. 112–15.

[7] A statistic shared by Prison Reform Trust: http://www.prisonreformtrust.org.uk/presspolicy/news/vw/1/itemID/494.

[8] 1 John 3:21–2.

[9] Carlos Whittaker, *Kill the Spider* (Grand Rapids, MI: Zondervan, 2017), p. 51.

[10] Richard Rohr, *The Wisdom Pattern* (Cincinnati, OH: Franciscan, 2001), p. 34.

[11] Luke 6:43–4.

[12] Rev. 3:2–3.

[13] John Sweet, *Revelation* (London: SCM Press, 1979), p. 98.

[14] Matt. 26:42.

[15] C. Griffin, *A Forgotten Revival: East Anglia and NE Scotland – 1921* (Leominster: Day One, 1992), pp. 113–18. www.dayone.co.uk.

12 - INTERCESSION AS INTERRUPTION

[1] From a prayer of Augustine and the title of a choral arrangement by Thomas Keesecker.

[2] https://www.opendoorsuk.org/news/latest-news/vian-iraq-care/ (accessed 11 Nov. 2023).

[3] Christians are now beginning to have new hope and see emotional healing. Open Doors, an international Christian ministry that provides a lifeline to persecuted Christians, is able to give practical and spiritual support, including trauma counselling programmes, medicine and relief through Centres of Hope.

[4] C.S. Lewis, *The Problem of Pain* (London: HarperCollins, 2012). © Copyright 1940 CS Lewis Pte Ltd. Extract used with permission.

[5] John 9:2.

[6] John 9:3.

[7] John 9:5.

[8] St Augustine, *Confessions* (trans. Benigus O-Rourke; London: Darton, Longman & Todd, 2014).

[9] Name changed to protect the person's identity.

[10] The Apple commercial was created by the advertising agency Chiat/Day, of Venice, California and helped to launch the hugely successful 'Think Different' campaign in 1997. https://www.youtube.com/watch?v=GEPhLqwKo6g (accessed 22 Dec. 2023).

[11] Taken from *The Life You Have Always Wanted* by John Ortberg (Grand Rapids, MI: Zondervan, 2002), pp. 92–3. Copyright © 2002 by John Ortberg. Used by permission of HarperCollins Christian Publishing.

[12] John 17:11–13.

[13] Rom. 8:34.

13 - STIR IT UP!

[1] A verse taken from Henry Wadsworth Longfellow's poem, 'To the River Charles', written in 1866. In H.W. Longfellow, *The Complete Works of Henry Wadsworth Longfellow* (Boston, MA: Ticknor & Fields).

[2] 1 Pet. 4:12, MSG.

3   2 Sam. 11 – 12.

4   1 Kgs 19:13.

5   John 7:37–9.

6   Richard Rohr, *The Wisdom Pattern* (Cincinnati, OH: Franciscan, 2020), p. 84.

7   Ezek. 47:7–10.

8   2 Cor. 5:21.

9   John 5:8.

10   1 Kgs 18:33–8.

11   Matt. 12:9–14.

12   Gal. 5:1.

13   St Augustine, *Return to Your Heart: Thoughts from St Augustine* (Compiled by Ben O'Rourke; Suffolk: Augustinian Press UK, 2015), p. 30.

14   St Ignatius, *The Spiritual Exercises of St. Ignatius* (Book-of-the-Month Club/Doubled, 1998).

15   1 Tim. 6:7.

16   Job 1:21.

14 – THE INTERRUPTION OF REST

1   Carey Nieuhoff, *Didn't See It Coming* (New York: Waterbrook, 2019), p. 104.

2   FOMO means 'fear of missing out'.

3   Generation Z is a social group for those born between 1997 and 2012 and so covers ages 16 to 24. Report published by GWI for the advertising industry in 2022.

4   Ps. 121:1.

5   Mark Sayer, *A Non-anxious Presence* (Chicago, IL: Moody, 2022).

6   George Orwell, *Animal Farm* (London: Penguin,1945).

7   Matt. 16:26.

8   Eccl. 3:7.

9   See Isa. 40:3.

10   Henri Nouwen, *The Way of the Heart* (London: HarperCollins, 1981), p. 66.

11   Credit Suisse Global Wealth Report, published in 2021.

Notes

12 Walter Brueggemann, *Sabbath as Resistance* (Kentucky: Westminster John Knox, 2017), pp. xiii–xiv.

13 Exod. 20:8–11.

14 Brueggemann, *Sabbath as Resistance*, p. 108.

15 Jas 3:17.

16 Jer. 29:11.

17 See John 3:16.

18 Can be found at https://hymnology.hymnsam.co.uk/a/alone-with-none-but-thee,-my-god (accessed 13 Oct. 2023).

EPILOGUE

1 Taken from the Queen's Christmas broadcast in 2002. The Queen had just celebrated her Golden Jubilee. It was also the year she had lost her mother and sister within a few weeks of each other.

2 Matt. 6:26–7.

3 Brother Andrew refers to this quote in his classic book, *God's Smuggler*, but it is thought to originate from a sermon preached by the English preacher, William Lonsdale Watkinson. See William Lonsdale Watkinson, 'Sermon XIV: The Invincible Strategy (Romans: xii, 21)', in *The Supreme Conquest and Other Sermons Preached in America by W.L. Watkinson* (New York: F.H. Revell, 1907).

4 W.H. Auden, 'Funeral Blues', in *The Collected Poems of W.H. Auden* (New York: Vintage Books, 1991). Copyright © 1940 by W.H. Auden, renewed. Reprinted by permission of Curtis Brown, Ltd. All rights reserved.

5 Mark 9:24.

6 1 Cor. 9:24.

7 Hymn: 'O Breath of Life', written by Elizabeth A.P. Head. © Mrs A.K. Charlton.

Hope Wins

How a vision of our eternal future impacts our lives today

Goff Hope

Hope is fundamental for human wellbeing but it is in short supply in our world. We can quickly be robbed of hope by illness, personal tragedy or by the sheer oppressive nature of news headlines.

Drawing on his own personal experiences, including the tragedy of losing his daughter and his own battle with cancer, Goff shares how holding on to the Christian hope of an eternal future transformed the darkest moments of his life.

Interweaving personal testimony of the goodness of God with biblical teaching on heaven, Goff encourages us to see that when tough times come, and we are tempted to doubt or ask the big questions, such as Why, Lord?, we can have hope if we keep our eyes on Jesus and have a heavenly perspective on life.

978-1-78893-276-9

When God 'Buts' In

Finding strength to face the impossible

Kate Williams

Are you facing a situation that looks impossible?

Many biblical characters faced huge obstacles too, until God brought a 'but' into the situation that changed their circumstances in a powerful way.

When God 'buts' in he isn't meddling or interfering, he is divinely intervening in the situation. Whether that results in a miraculous turnaround in circumstances or grace to sustain you through a trial, God wants to 'but' in and be actively involved in your life.

Kate Williams interweaves her personal experience of challenge with biblical truth to help stir your faith and trust in God.

978-1-78893-308-7

Authentic

We trust you enjoyed reading this book from Authentic. If you want to be informed of any new titles from this author and other releases you can sign up to the Authentic newsletter by scanning below:

Online:
authenticmedia.co.uk

Follow us: